STUFFLEBEEM,
BROCKWAY
& STURT

The Origins
of Our Surnames

SHELLEY KLEIN

MICHAEL O'MARA BOOKS LIMITED

First published in Great Britain in 2002 by
Michael O'Mara Books Limited
9 Lion Yard, Tremadoc Road
London SW4 7NQ

A CIP catalogue record for this book is available
from the British Library

ISBN 1-85479-864-2

1 3 5 7 9 10 8 6 4 2

Designed and typeset by Martin Bristow

Printed and bound in Finland by WS Bookwell, Juva

Introduction

HE STUDY of British, Australian and American surnames is neither a precise nor a simple one. Over the centuries, there have been so many variable factors, not the least of which was the disinclination of our forebears to spell consistently, that it is hardly an exact science. However, having said this, there *are* four different categories that most surnames fall into, which do make research a little easier and certainly a lot more comprehensive.

First, there is the patronymic surname – i.e. those that derived from the bearer's ancestors or from their family or clan members. **Janson**, for instance, means 'son of John', while **Stevenson** means 'son of Stephen'. There are so many instances of such names – **Adamson**, **Jackson**, **Peterson**, etc. – that many have had to be omitted from this book, but their meaning is in any case perfectly obvious. The patronymic surname did not really become established until after the Norman Conquest (except in the Celtic fringes of the British Isles, as mentioned below).

Second, there is the 'toponymic' – the name deriving from a locality, usually the place from which a man came, or where he owned land. This is a large group (in fact probably the largest of the four), encompassing as it does not only the names of towns and villages, for example **York** and **Longford**, but also a huge number of smaller localities incorporating minute local information such as soil-type – whether somewhere was stony or marshy, whether someone lived near to an oak wood or a bridge made from ash trees, whether a field was ploughed or uncultivated. Thus, **Denleigh** means a 'dweller by a clearing in a valley', and **Aschcombe** means someone who lives in or near an ash-tree valley, while nearly all names that include 'beck' or 'brook' refer to streams or rivers. (Trees and physical characteristics of the land feature highly in surnames.) In fact, the list is inexhaustible and the more you research the subject, the more you see what a multitude of possibilities there is.

Third, there is the occupational or 'office' name. It is supposed that up to twenty per cent of all our surnames derive from this group – for instance, **Prior**, **Page**, **Sergeant** or **Baker** – but it is worth bearing in mind that some words do not mean the same thing today as they did originally. A farmer, for example, was a person who had the right to collect tax, or rent – a tax-collector or bailiff – from the Old French, *ferme*, meaning rented land. Some apparently occupational names, however, fall into our fourth category, that of nicknames – for instance, **Nun** might be someone who was nun-like in their appearance or behaviour (which must be more likely than occupational, if you think about it . . .), or **Lord** ('as proud as a lord'), or **Lamb** ('as meek as a lamb'). Some occupational names might equally be place names – **Bridger**, for example, could mean a 'keeper of the bridge/someone who collects the tolls', or someone who lived close to a bridge.

As a social document, occupational names are also of great historical interest, recording as they do several professions that no longer exist. A **Habbeshaw**, for example, was a maker of hauberks (chain-mail coats), while a **Slaymaker** was a maker of an instrument used in weaving.

Fourth, as already mentioned, there are the nicknames. Most commonly these started off as descriptions (not always polite – it is a wonder that some of them survived) of the original bearer's physical appearance – his hair colour, how tall or short he was, how ugly he was, any distinguishing feature he might have had – but also, on occasion, his foibles, disposition, or, indeed, moral fibre. Thus, the first **Redhead**, and the first **Russell**, probably had red hair (if not, then a red face); **Gulliver** was a glutton (from Old French *goulafre*); **Froud** (from Old English *frōd*) was prudent, and **Fairweather** was someone with a sunny disposition.

Animal names were also often applied as nicknames; **Lark** was someone with a sweet voice, **Crane** had long, skinny legs, **Lamb** had a meek temperament, while **Bull** would be quite the opposite.

Of course, within all of these groups there is a great deal of overlapping. A place name can also apply to someone's occupation and vice-versa, or a name used as a nickname might also be an occupational name – **Lamb**, for example, could also be someone who tended lambs. In addition to this there can also be two or three different meanings to the same name: e.g. **Court** could derive from Middle English and mean 'someone who lived or worked at a large manor house', or it could come from Old French and mean 'someone who was short in stature'. Similarly, **Pike**, can have a number of derivations: the Old English *pīc* meaning 'hilltop', 'point' (as in a conical hill or as in the fish, which has a long, pointed snout) or 'pickaxe' – so the original bearer might have lived near a pointed hill, or been a pikeman; the Old French meaning 'woodpecker' (perhaps he was a carpenter); or the Middle English for 'pike', in this case the fish – so perhaps the original person caught and/or sold freshwater fish. This, of course, means that accurate classification into one of the four groups is well nigh impossible, but the thing to remember is that our ancestors, far from being concerned with hard-and-fast rules, were more interested in identifying their neighbours quickly and with ease – so they used whatever came to hand. In addition to this, with the influx of so many different cultures – Germanic and Norse, Roman, Norman – several languages were also incorporated. The various Germanic invasions (those of the Jutes, Saxons, Angles, followed by the Vikings, Danes, Norwegians), from AD 400 onwards, led to names referring, for instance, to wolves, eagles, fairies and elves. Even after the Norman Conquest in 1066 the Germanic influence didn't cease to exist, as the Normans were 'North men' (in fact ultimately of Danish descent) and as such their own language had a touch of Scandinavian to it. That being said, the Norman Conquest did bring with it one major difference. Up until that point surnames, rather than being passed on from generation to generation as they are now, were tailored to fit the individual. After the Norman Conquest, however, the fixed, hereditary surname became firmly rooted (as it was in the Scottish Highlands or Ireland, where the Gaelic patronymic system was already in operation using prefixes such as **Mac**, **Mc**, **M'** and **Ó** to show descent). Whatever the case, the coming of the Normans certainly gave impetus to the fixed hereditary principle and after two or three generations Norman names (such as William,

Robert, Richard, Walter, etc.) had largely superseded the Old English ones. Some names led to many other surnames being coined: Richard, for instance, gave rise to Ritchie, Ricketts, Dickson, Dixon, Hick, Rick, and more . . .

The American surname is no less of a jumble. Proud to have been (and still to be) a melting pot of many different cultures, North America's colourful history is reflected in its surnames. The first European language to be widely spoken in what is now the United States was English, but until the Civil War in 1860 the Western States were largely populated by either the Irish or Germans, after which there followed an influx of various nationalities from Slavs to Italians, from Scandinavians to Dutch, from Poles to French. Over time, some of these European names were anglicized – sometimes in spelling as well as pronunciation – to emphasize their bearers' status as Americans (for instance, the father of the former US Vice-President Spiro Agnew changed his name to Agnew from Anagnostopoulos on his arrival from Greece). Other immigrants to the USA either did not see the point of doing so, or perhaps felt that their surname was the one bit of 'the old country' they could pass down from generation to generation. Some of these names are included in this book, which, however, concentrates for the most part on the oldest surnames of that nation – those that derive from the British shores. To a lesser extent, perhaps, Australia has followed a similar 'name history'.

As mentioned above, the most obvious of the patronymics have, for the sake of space, been omitted. For the same reason, a number of those arising from specific locations – such as **London**, **Worcester**, **Hampshire**, etc. – have had to be left out. In a number of cases, names have been grouped together when they share a derivation and prefix – thus **Ackford** or **Acton** may be found in the entry for **Acfield**. But there are many thousands of surnames, and only a fraction can be included in this book. Those disappointed not to find their names here might nevertheless be able to work out the meaning of their name from the derivations of other, similar names included here. It might also be worth bearing in mind that as well as there being many variant spellings among British names, in Scotland and, particularly, Ireland, the prefixes **Mac, Mc, M'** (all 'son of') and **O'** (**Ó** – 'grandson of') were in some cases dropped in a process of 'Englishing', while in many cases Gaelic spellings were simplified and anglicized as well (occasionally they were translated – thus an Irishman called MacAteer might become known as Carpenter). In recent years an opposing trend – again notably in Ireland – is evident, as people revert to the Gaelic forms of their names, leaving the English at a loss as to how to pronounce them.

Whatever the origin and meaning of your surname, I do hope you enjoy dipping into this book and take as much fun out of the subject as I have had pleasure researching it.

SHELLEY KLEIN
May 2002

A BRIEF NOTE ON THE SOURCE LANGUAGES

Where the originating language is concerned, for the sake of simplicity, only the most immediate source is generally given – therefore in most cases if a word comes from, say, Old French but via Middle English, only Middle English is cited. It has to be remembered that in England the language spoken during the centuries before the Norman Conquest (that is, from around the fifth century AD until the mid-eleventh to the twelfth) was Old English (also called Anglo-Saxon), which included, as well as Saxon words (from western Germany) and a number of local dialects, a fair bit of Old Norse, introduced by the Vikings (Old Norse itself was a mixture of Scandinavian dialects, including Old Icelandic). Although some words are recognizable, Old English tends to sound very foreign to modern English ears. (Old French, a less ancient language, dating from about the ninth century to the fifteenth, resembles Modern French much more closely than Old English resembles Modern English.) Following the Norman Conquest, Old English absorbed a number of Old French words, and gradually evolved into what is called Middle English, which is usually dated from about 1100. By the middle of the fifteenth century it was beginning to develop into Modern English.

Abb, Abba, Abbe, Abbey, Abbs, Abby from Old French, meaning 'abbot' – and probably a nickname, rather than occupational, although it could also have been given to someone who worked at an abbey. In some cases, however, the name might have been a diminutive form of either 'Abel' or 'Abraham'.

Abbatt, Abbott, Abbotts from Old English, meaning 'abbot', or sometimes as a diminutive of Abraham – 'little Abraham'. The *s* of 'Abbotts' could indicate a servant of an abbot.

Abel, Abell, Abele, Abeles, Able the name of the first murder victim – a common Christian name in the thirteenth and fourteenth centuries – is from the Hebrew *Abel* meaning 'son'. (So presumably **Abelson**, 'son of Abel', could be translated as 'son-son'.)

Abercrombie, Abercromby Scots Gaelic in origin – from Abercromby in Fife – meaning 'mouth of the crooked stream'.

Ablewhite *see* **Applewhaite** (under **Apperley**).

Abraham, Abrahams, Abram, Abrams, Abrahamson, Abramson from the Hebrew, meaning 'father of a multitude', or 'high father'. Not confined to people of the Jewish faith.

Acfield from Old English, meaning 'open country with oaks'. Similarly, **Acford** or **Ackford** means 'ford at the oaks'; **Acland** or **Ackland** is 'land where oaks grew'; **Ackroyd, Ecroyd** 'dweller by the oak clearing'; **Acton, Aughton**, 'place at the oak(s)', and **Ayckbourn** means 'stream in the oaks'. The names could have been given to people who lived at such places, or to someone who came from a place that had one of the names.

Acheson, Aicheson, Aitcheson, Aitchison, Atcheson, Atchison Scots and Border forms of **Atkinson** (*see* **Atkin**).

Acker, Ackers, Ackerman, Acraman, Acreman, Acres, Akerman, Akers, Akess, Akker from the Old English, meaning 'pasture or arable', thus applied to someone who dwelt by a plot of arable land, or, with the suffix '-man', a farmer – i.e. 'plot man, husbandman or ploughman'.

Adam, Adames, Adams, Addams from the Hebrew, meaning 'man' – although some sources claim that the name is from the Hebrew for 'red'. Adam became a very popular Christian name during the thirteenth century, and spawned a number of surnames. **Addis** is thought to be a diminutive form of Adam. In Scotland and Ireland, especially, the name sometimes appears as **Addy, Adie** or **Eadie**, from which comes the name **Addison**, which is therefore the same name as **Adamson**. (*See also* **Atkin**.)

Affleck from Scots Gaelic, meaning 'field of flat stone'. The original bearers are most likely to have come either from the lands of Auchinleck in Ayrshire, or from Affleck in Angus. Over time – and with the aid of the uncertain spellings of the thirteenth and fourteenth centuries, the two names came to be pronounced similarly. The name survives as Affleck and as Auchinleck. The latter is sometimes pronounced 'Affleck'.

Agate, Agates nothing to do with the gemstone, but a compression of the Old English for 'at the gate'– a name for someone who either lived at a gate or at a residence near the gate, possibly the town gate – or was a gatekeeper or porter (as today the doorman of, say, an hotel might be referred to by the other workers at the hotel as 'Jim at the door' to distinguish him from 'Jim at the reception desk'). (*See also* **Yate, Yates**.)

Agnew probably from Old French, meaning 'lamb': as with the name **Lamb** it was probably a nickname the original bearer earned through mildness of temperament. It is occasionally used as an anglicization of the Irish name Ó Gnímh.

Airey, Airy, Eyrye, Eyree probably from Old Norse, meaning 'gravel-bank river', and was a name given to someone who lived by a gravel bank.

Aitken, Aitkens, Aitkin, Aitkins all Scottish forms of the name **Atkin(s)** (*see below*).

Alabastar, Alabaster, from Old French, meaning 'a soldier armed with a crossbow'. (*See also* **Ballester.**)

Alan, Allain, Allen, Alleyne, etc. could have come from the Breton Saint Alan, or, especially in Scotland, from the Gaelic word for 'rock', when it would probably have been given to someone who was as 'steadfast as a rock'.

Alaway, Allway, Alloway, Halloway and other variants could be from Old English, meaning either 'noble war' or 'elf war'.

Alban, Aubon from the Latin *alba* meaning 'white'. Alba was the name of a city in both Italy and Gaul and so the surname can also mean 'from Alba'. In either case, it probably originated in the time of Roman Britain.

Albert, Allberts, Aubert from Old English, meaning 'noble bright' (the prefix *Ad-* in other names might also signify 'noble'). The name **Albright** or **Allbright** has probably the same meaning.

Alcott, Allcott, Aucott, Aucutt from Old English meaning someone who lived in an 'old cottage/hut'. Similarly, the name **Allchurch** would probably have been given to someone who lived near an 'old church'.

Alden, Auden, Olden might be from Old English, meaning 'old friend'. Or it might, like **Haldane** and its variants, be a version of the Scandinavian name Hálfdan, meaning 'half Dane'.

Alder, Alders, Older from Old English, meaning, quite simply 'someone who lives close by/next to alder trees'. **Alderman,** on the other hand, is an occupational name and would have been applied to someone who was a headman or governor of a guild, the prefix 'Alder' here coming from the Old English word for 'elder' – as in a 'church elder', etc.

Aldred possibly from Old English, meaning 'old counsel', though whether this was a first name, a nickname originally given to some 'old chap' who was always giving advice, or to someone who only ever gave old or outdated advice, or whether it has some other source, is far from clear.

Aldrich, **Aldridge**, **Eldridge**, **Oldridge** and other variants, probably from Old English meaning 'elf ruler', 'noble ruler', or 'old ruler'.

Alexander from Greek, meaning a 'defender of men'. How it came to be a surname is uncertain, but it was probably a patronymic. A diminutive form is **Sanders**, and it is also found in **MacAllister** ('son of Alexander') in Scotland.

Alfred, **Alfreds**, **Allured** from Old English, meaning 'elf counsel' or possibly 'noble counsel'. The latter seems less likely, if only because Alfred the Great's older brother was called Æthelred, which has the same meaning. (Famously, a later King Æthelred came in more recent times to be called, inaccurately, 'the Unready' – his nickname was in fact *Unræd*, meaning 'without counsel', a reflection of how his subjects saw his rule.)

Algar, **Elgar** from Old English, meaning 'elf spear' or 'old spear'. A similar pair of derivations can be found for the names **Alston**, **Allstone**, meaning 'old stone' or 'elf stone'. Likewise, such names as **Alwin**, **Alwen**, **Allwyn**, **Aylwin**, **Elvin** might mean either 'old friend' or 'elf friend' . . . though they could also be from another word, meaning 'noble friend'.

Alis, **Allis**, **Hallis** from Old German, meaning 'noble kind'. Nowadays, when used as a first name, the name is spelled 'Alice'. The diminutive form, **Alison**, **Allison**, was very common in England and Scotland from the thirteenth to the seventeenth centuries. The original forms and their diminutives came to be used as surnames.

Other 'noble' surnames with the prefix 'Al-' or 'All-' include **Almond** meaning 'noble protector'; **Allnatt**, **Allnutt** meaning 'noble boldness'; **Alsop**, **Allsep**, **Allsopp**, etc., meaning 'noble valley'; **Aylmer**, **Elmer**, etc. meaning 'noble-famous'; **Alward**, **Elward** meaning 'elf guard', and **Aylward**, probably meaning 'noble guard', but which could also be 'elf guard'. To add further confusion, **Almond** might be yet another variant spelling of a name which comes in many versions, including **Alman**, **Allman**, **Almon**, **Allamond**, **Aliment**, and derives from Old French meaning 'German'.

Allmark, **Hallmark** probably derived from a nickname meaning 'half a mark', a reflection of the original bearer's financial status, perhaps.

Ambler from Old French, meaning either 'enameller', or an 'ambling horse' and applied to people with an ambling gait.

Ambrose from Greek, meaning 'divine/immortal'.

Amery, **Emery**, **Imbery**, **Imrie**, and other variants, are all from Old German, meaning 'work-rule'.

Ames, **Amis**, **Amos** from Latin, meaning 'friend' – this word was often used as a term for the lower classes and slaves. The biblical name of **Amos** came into use in England after the Reformation.

Anders, **Andrewes**, **Andrews**, are forms of **Andrew**, which is from Greek, meaning 'manly', and is the name of the first of Jesus' disciples. His bones were brought to Scotland, where he is patron saint. As a surname, however, **Andrew** is most widespread in Devon and Cornwall. **Anderson** quite simply means 'son of Andrew'.

Angus from the Irish and Scots Gaelic, meaning 'unique choice'. As a surname it could stem either from the forename Angus, or from the district of that name. As a first name it has sometimes been turned into the Classical-sounding Æneas. **MacGuinness** and **MacInnes** are, respectively, the Irish and Scots patronymics meaning 'son of Angus', whereas **Angusson** is an 'Englishing' of the patronymic.

Ansell, **Hansell**, along with a number of other variants, are from Old German, meaning 'god-helmet'.

Anstruther a local Fife name deriving from Scots Gaelic, meaning 'the stream'.

Apperley, Apperly from 'apple' and the Old English word for 'wood or clearing'. There are many Apple names: **Applebe, Applebee, Applebey, Appleby** meaning an 'apple farm' and denoting someone who either lived or worked on one; **Applegarth, Applegath, Applegate** from Old Norse, meaning a 'dwelling near an apple orchard', and **Appleton** from Old English, meaning much the same (and, from it, **Napleton**); **Applewhaite, Applewhite, Ablewhite** mean 'apple wood/clearing', and **Appleyard** means just what it sounds like.

April, Averill, Avril from Old French, meaning 'April'. It was probably a nickname given to those with changeable temperaments like the month, or it might refer to those born in that month.

Archbald, Archbold, Archibald, Archibold, Archibould from Old German, meaning 'precious bold'. **Archibald** is a common first name in Scotland.

Arden from Old English, meaning 'dwelling place' or 'gravel valley'.

Arkwright from Old English, meaning a maker of arks, or chests.

Arlott, Arlotte from Old French, meaning 'vagabond, fellow, rogue'. The original of 'harlot', it was applicable to both men and women and not necessarily derogatory. It was, for instance, used by Chaucer both as a term of derision and to mean a good fellow. The modern sense of the word 'harlot' is not found until after the fifteenth century.

Armistead, Armstead from Old French, meaning 'hermit' plus the Old English word for 'place' – thus meaning someone who lives in or near a hermitage. **Armitage** from the Old French for 'hermitage' has the same meaning.

Armstrong a name which means exactly what it suggests, and was doubtless given to the local strong man.

Arnald, **Arnold**, **Arnall**, **Arnott**, **Harnott**, and further variants, from Old German, meaning 'eagle-power'. **Arneway** is thought to come from Old English, meaning 'eagle-warrior'.

Arthur is most likely to come from the Greek for 'bear guardian'. Celtic sources also relate the name Arthur to 'bear' and also to 'stone'. Famously, of course, the name belonged to the legendary hero-king, of Knights of the Round Table fame.

Ash, **Asch**, **Asche**, **Ashe**, **Aske**, etc. from Old English, meaning 'ash tree', stands on its own or as a prefix in a number of surnames. On its own the name **Ash** was probably bestowed on a person who lived near or among ash trees, and it could be the source of other surnames such as **Dash**, **Hash**, **Lash**, **Nash**, **Rash**, **Tash**. In combination with another word, **Ash** names include **Ashbridge** meaning 'bridge at the ash tree'; **Ashbrook** would be the name given to someone who lived in a place where there was a brook and ash trees (but it could also be from 'eastern brook'); **Ashby**, **Ashbee** from Old Norse, meaning an 'ash-tree farm'; **Ashcombe** would have been someone living in or near to an 'ash-tree valley'; **Ashcroft** would have been someone who lived in a 'croft among ash trees'; **Asher** was someone who lived near or amidst ash trees. The original bearers of the names **Ashfield**, **Ashfold**, **Ashford** and **Ashwood** all came from such topographical landmarks, all with ash trees, while **Ashley** means 'ash-tree wood or clearing', and **Ashton** a 'place where there are ash trees'.

Ashman, from Old English, meaning a sailor or even pirate, though it certainly seems possible that it might also have been given to a man who lived near or among ash trees.

Aspell, from Old English meaning someone dwelling on either 'land with aspens growing on it' or a 'hill with aspens'.

Aspinal, **Aspinall**, **Aspinwall** from Old English, meaning 'a stream in the aspens', and therefore relating to someone who lived near one.

Atcheson, **Atchison** *see* **Atkin**.

Atkin, **Atkins**, **Adkins** from a diminutive of **Adam** – 'Ad-kin'. It also appears as **Aitken**, **Aitkins**, etc. The patronymic **Atkinson** appears in many forms – **Acheson**, **Aitcheson**, **Atchison**, etc.

Attenborough from Old English, meaning 'at the grove' or 'at the mound, hill or fort'. The prefix 'At-' (or 'Atte-') in surnames often means 'at' or 'by' – thus **Athill**, **Atthill**, **Athell** would be 'someone who lives by the hill'; **Attlee**, **Attley** 'at the wood'; **Attwell** means 'someone who lives by a spring or stream', and **Attwood**, **Atwood**, 'someone who lives by the wood'.

Aubray, **Aubrey**, **Aubry**, and other variants, from Old German, probably either meaning 'elf ruler', or 'elf counsel'.

Auchinleck *see* **Affleck**.

Auchmuty, **Achmuty** from the region of that name in Fife, the Scots Gaelic meaning a 'muddy field or swine pen'.

Auden *see* **Alden**.

Austen, **Austin**, **Austins**, **Auston** very likely to be a diminutive form of the name **Augustine** – the Augustinian Friars are sometimes called the Austin Friars.

Averill, **Avril** *see* April.

Ayckbourn *see under* **Acfield**.

Bach, **Bache**, **Batch** from Old English, meaning 'stream' and so given to someone who lived near a stream. (*See also* **Beck**.)

Backer and **Baiker** are variant spellings of **Baker**, which means just that – someone who was a baker. **Bagster** or **Baxter** – as in the food company famous for its soups – probably derives from the Old English feminine form of 'baker'.

Backhouse, from Old English meaning 'bakehouse', would have been given to someone who worked in a bakery – also a baker (*see above*), or maybe a baker's assistant. It is sometimes spelled **Baccas** or **Bacchus** – perhaps disappointingly for those who bear this name, it has nothing to do with the Greek god Bacchus.

Bacon, **Bakon** from Middle English, meaning exactly that, though also a side of ham and, occasionally, fresh pork. Probably an occupational name given to a butcher, specifically a pork butcher.

Badger, **Badgers**, **Bagger** from Middle English, meaning a 'bag or a small sack', so 'a maker of bags'. On the other hand, if originating from the late fifteenth century and after, the name could mean 'hawker or huckster'. In neither case has the name anything to do with the animal, which until the sixteenth century was usually known as a 'brock'.

Badman contrary to expectation, this name does not mean 'a bad man' but comes from Middle English, meaning a 'beadsman' or man of God who prayed for the soul for another, usually for a fee or board and lodging. The name is also spelled **Beadman**.

Badrick, **Betteridge**, and other variants, come from Old English, meaning 'battle-powerful'.

Bagg, **Bagge**, **Baggs** this surname was very popular in Middle English and probably refers to a 'maker of bags'; however, it might also have been applied to a beggar.

Bail, **Baile**, **Bailes**, **Bails**, **Bale**, **Bales**, **Bayles** from Middle English, meaning a 'bailey' – the outer wall or court of a castle. The original bearer of this name would probably have been someone who guarded the outer court.

Bailey, **Bayley**, **Bayliss** probably from Old French, meaning a 'bailiff', rather than yet another variant of **Bail** above.

Bain, **Baine**, **Baines**, **Baynes** this name could derive as a nickname from the Scots Gaelic for 'fair, white', or from Old English for 'bone' (which in the North and in Scotland came to be pronounced 'bane', but further south turned into 'bone'). When in the singular it might also derive from the Old Norse, meaning 'direct' or 'ready to serve'. Another possible source is Middle English, meaning 'bath' and might have been the occupational name of someone who worked at a public baths.

Bainbridge from Old Norse, meaning a 'direct or straight bridge', perhaps denoting someone who lived close to one – or someone who came from Bainbridge in Yorkshire.

Bakewell from Old English, meaning 'stream' and 'spring': probably referring to someone who lived near the source of a stream.

Bald, **Bauld**, probably from Old English, meaning 'bold'; it could, however, also derive from Middle English, meaning 'round' or 'corpulent'; or 'bald-headed'. **Balding** and **Boulding**, however, have nothing to do with baldness – they are variants of **Baldwin** (*see below*).

Baldwin, **Balwin**, **Balding**, **Boulding** from Old English, meaning a 'bold friend'.

Balfour from Scots Gaelic, meaning a 'village with a meadow', but the name might refer to someone from lands of that name in Fife.

Ball, Balle, Balls there are various sources for this name including the Old English for a 'round hill' or the Middle English meaning 'bald place' or 'round one'. It could therefore have been given as a nickname to a plump person, or to someone with a smooth round head, or to someone who lived near a round hill. **Baller** probably means either someone who made balls or someone who lived near a rounded hill.

Ballard from Middle English, meaning a 'bald-headed man'.

Ballaster, Ballester, Ballister, Balster from Old French, meaning a 'crossbow man'.

Bamford from Old English, meaning someone who dwelt near a 'ford by a bean field'. Similarly, **Bamfield** would have been someone from a place of that name or someone who lived by a bean field, and **Bancroft** probably means that the original bearer of the name lived in a croft, or cottage, by a field of beans.

Bank, Banker, Bankes from Middle English, meaning 'mound of earth, ridge, or riverbank' would have been someone who lived on or by a bank or ridge of earth, a hillside, or a riverbank.

Bann of uncertain origin, it could derive from Middle English, meaning 'proclamation' (as in 'banns'), and was perhaps given to someone authorized to make announcements, such as a town-crier, or to a renowned gossip, perhaps; or it might come from Old French, meaning 'hamper, pannier', given as a name to a maker of these, a basket-maker (*see* **Bannister** *below*). If of Irish origin, the name could mean someone who lived by either of two rivers called Bann – one in Coleraine, Northern Ireland; and the other in County Wexford in the Republic.

Bannister, Bannester, Banister from Old French, meaning a 'basket', it would have been given to a basket-maker.

Bannerman means exactly that – 'the man who carries the banner'. It is mainly found in Scotland.

Barber, Barbour from Old French, meaning 'barber'. The original bearer was not necessarily a cutter of hair and trimmer of beards, however – barbers were known also to perform dentistry and surgery.

Barclay, **Berkeley**, **Berkley** from Old English, meaning 'birchwood', indicating someone who resided in or near one.

Barfield, **Barford** from Old English, meaning 'barley', hence a name given to someone who lived by a field of barley, or near a ford by a barley field. **Barley** might originally have been someone who grew barley, or who made and/or sold barley-bread. **Barwick** and **Berwick** mean someone who lived or worked at a 'barley farm'; **Barlow(e)** for someone who lived by a 'barley hill' or 'sloping field of barley'. Another barley-derived name is **Barton**, meaning barley farm.

Barker, **Berker** either from Middle English, meaning 'tanner' – that is, someone who stripped bark from trees and tanned it (often for use in saddle-making), or from Old French, meaning 'shepherd'.

Barnes from Old English, meaning someone who lived in, at, or near a 'barn, barley house'.

Baron, **Barron** from Old French, denoting the rank of 'baron', but sometimes applied as a nickname to someone from the lower classes who was as haughty and proud as a baron.

Barrat, **Barrett**, **Barritt**, **Barrott** it is thought most likely that this is a nickname from Middle English, meaning 'trade and commerce', which came to mean 'trouble' or 'fraud'. Or it could be derived from the Old French for 'cap' and refer to someone whose occupation was as hatmaker.

Base, **Bass** from Middle English, for someone who is short, of low stature. **Basset** and **Bassett** are diminutives of 'bass', and mean the same – or possibly refer to a *very* short person.

Bastard from Old French, meaning exactly that. In certain state documents William the Conqueror was referred to as 'William the Bastard', so it was not necessarily seen as pejorative.

Beach, **Beech** from Old English, meaning either 'stream' or 'beech tree', and applied to someone who lived by one or the other.

Beecher, Becher, Beechman from Old English, and all denoting someone who lived by a beech tree. **Beechey** means 'one who lives by a beech enclosure'. **Beecham**, on the other hand, a name made famous by the conductor Sir Thomas and his family's renowned pills, is an anglicized spelling of the French **Beauchamp** – 'beautiful field' – and probably originated in places of that name in France, brought over with the Normans and later. Other variants are **Beachamp**, **Beacham**, **Beachem**. (**Beaumont** has a similar French source – 'beautiful mountain' – but is pronounced 'Bo-' rather than 'Bee-'.)

Beadel, Beadell, Beadle, Beadles from Old English, meaning a 'beadle' or 'town-crier'. Among the many variants of this name are **Bedell**, **Biddle** and **Buddles**.

Beal, Beale, Beales from Old French, meaning 'beautiful', possibly a nickname, otherwise meaning someone from a place of that name, e.g. in Northumberland.

Beaves, Beavis, Bovis from French for 'beloved or fine son' (*beau/ bel fils*).

Beck from Old Norse, meaning 'a stream'; it could have denoted someone who lived near a stream, or people coming from places of that or similar names – such as various places called Bec in France. Alternatively, it might have come from Old French, and been a nickname given perhaps to someone with a long pointed nose – a beak. Or it could have come from Old English, meaning 'pickaxe, mattock' – and have been applied to a maker or seller of these. **Beckett** is most likely a diminutive of 'beak'.

Beckham it seems most likely that here the 'Beck' prefix means 'stream, brook' and in conjunction with the Old English word for 'a piece of low-lying, flat land near a stream' would have indicated someone who lived on such a piece of land. Alternatively, the second syllable could mean 'abode, village' – indicating someone who lived in a house or village near a stream.

Bell like **Beal** probably from Old French, meaning 'beautiful', but it could also be an occupational name, referring to a bellman or town-crier, or a bellringer. It could also have been the name given to someone who lived next to a bell-tower or a church noted for its bells, or by an inn called the Bell.

Bellamy from Old French, meaning a 'fair friend'.

Bellman, **Belman** from Old English, meaning a 'bellman' i.e. a town-crier. Or it could come from Old French *bele* plus *man* to make 'fair man' – a half-translated form of the name **Belham**, which is derived from the Old French *bel homme*.

Benbow, **Benbough** from Middle English, meaning literally 'bend bow' and therefore applied to an archer.

Benet, **Bennett** is usually a diminutive of Benedict, from *benedictus*, meaning 'blessed'; **Benson** as a rule means 'son of Benedict'.

Bent from Middle English, meaning 'stiff grass', so this name generally indicated someone who lived near a grassy area, heathland.

Berriman, **Berryman** from Middle English, meaning a 'servant at the manor house'. **Berry**, **Bury** from Old English for 'fort' or from Middle English for 'manor house' would have usually had the same meaning of servant at the big house, though might also have been applied to someone who lived next to a fort.

Best, **Beste** perhaps disappointingly for those who have this surname, it does not mean that they are 'the best'. It is taken from Old French, meaning beast and was usually a name given to someone with a nasty and violent temperament, or possibly a dull-witted cow-like person. On occasion the name might have applied to someone who looked after animals, a farmworker in charge of the sheep or cattle, say.

Birch, **Burch** from Old English, meaning 'birch', indicating one who lived near birch trees. Other birch surnames include **Burchill** for someone living near a 'birch-covered hill'; **Birchett** ('birch head') meaning a 'dweller by a birch-covered headland'; and **Birkenshaw** for someone who lived in or by a 'birch wood'.

Bish, **Bysh**, **Bysshe** from Old English, meaning 'thicket', indicating someone who dwelt near one. Percy Bysshe Shelley is the most famous bearer of that name.

Black, **Blacke** from Old English meaning someone who was dark-haired or of dark complexion. There are numerous 'Black' names, which may be assumed to indicate that something was black – but it is well to recognize that the Old English word for 'clear, bright, pale, shining' was *blāc*, and some confusion between the two words developed over the centuries. **Blackbourn** is more likely to mean 'black stream', just as **Blackstock** must be 'black stump' and **Blackwell** 'black spring or stream' – and, as surnames, indicate people who lived near such features, or came from places with those names. But the lengthened 'a' in **Blake** and **Blakelock** might indicate either a person who was dark, or one who was pale; dark-haired or blond or grey-haired.

Blair a Scots name, referring to someone coming from one of the several places of that name in Scotland. It became a well-known name in parts of Northern Ireland.

Blewett, **Blewitt**, **Blouet**, **Bluett** from Old French, meaning 'blue/bluish'. Presumably a nickname, although it is unclear to what it referred – someone whose hair was so black it looked blue? Or, more likely, a dyer whose hands and arms were stained a bluish colour through contact with dyes.

Bly, **Blythe**, **Bligh** from Old English, meaning 'merry, pleasant, cheerful'.

Bloomer, **Blomer**, **Blumer** from Old English, meaning 'iron ingot' – therefore applied to an iron-worker. In the case of **Bloomingdale's** – the famous New York department store – however, the name is possibly the anglicization of German 'Blumental', meaning a 'valley of flowers'.

Blond, **Blunt**, **Blount** from Old French, meaning 'blond' or 'fair-haired'. **Blondell**, **Blundell** are diminutive forms.

Bolt, **Bolte**, **Boult** from Old English, meaning a 'bolt, bar'. It could have been applied either to someone who was short and stocky in appearance, or to a maker of bolts. **Bolter** and **Boulter** also probably referred to a maker of bolts, although they could come from Old French, meaning a 'sifter of meal'.

Bond, Bound, Bondi, Bundy (and a number of other variants) from Old English, meaning a 'peasant' or 'serf' or 'bondservant'.

Bone, Bonn, Bunn from Old French, meaning 'good': as surnames the following must all have been nicknames: **Bonamy** 'good friend'; **Bonar** (and variants, including **Bonney** like the outlaw Billy the Kid) meaning 'pleasant, courteous'; **Bonham** 'good man'.

Booth, Boothe from Middle English, meaning 'hut, shelter, bothy' referring to someone living in such a hut, or – as the shelters were often for the use of herdsmen – a shepherd or cowherd. **Boothby** and **Boothroyd** are most likely to have been names given to people from the places called by those names (in Lincolnshire or Yorkshire, for example).

Borden possibly from Old English, meaning either 'boar valley' or 'boar hill', and referring to someone who lived in or by a valley or hill where boars roamed.

Borrell, Borrill *see* **Burrel**

Bosanquet a name that came to Britain in the sixteenth century with the French Protestants, the Huguenots, fleeing persecution. It is thought to originate with the Languedoc word meaning 'dwarf'.

Botham, Bothams, Bottom, Bottome, Bottoms, Bottams from Old English, meaning 'the lowest part of a valley', and applied to someone who dwelt in such a place. For obvious reasons, the spelling and pronunciation used by the cricketer Ian Botham are preferred. **Bottomley** denoted someone who lived in a wood at the bottom of a valley.

Bough, Bow, Bowes from Old English, meaning 'curved'; it probably referred to someone living near arches, or an arched bridge.

Bowden, Bowdin, Bowdon possibly from Old English, meaning a 'curved hill'. Someone from one of the places called by these names.

Bowie from Scots Gaelic, meaning a 'yellow-haired' person.

Boycott possibly deriving from the Old French for 'wood' plus the Old English for 'cottage', the name may have referred to a small cottage in a wood; however, it seems most likely that as a surname it was applied to people who came from one of the places of that name, in Buckinghamshire and Shropshire. The word 'boycott' comes from a Captain Charles Cunningham Boycott, a nineteenth-century British land agent in County Mayo who refused to lower rents and tried to evict tenants during a time of famine. They demonstrated their dismay by avoiding having anything at all to do with him – thus was created the verb 'to boycott', which in the course of time has also become used as a noun.

Bradbury from Old English, meaning 'broad fort' or a large manor house, and applied to someone living or employed at such a place. There are a number of 'Broad-' surnames, including **Bradfield** for a dweller in 'broad, open land'; **Bradley** someone living in a 'broad clearing in a wood'; **Bradman** for a 'broad man'; **Bradstreet** for someone who lived on a 'broad street'; and **Bradwell** meaning someone who lived by a 'broad spring or stream'.

Branagh, **Brannagh**, **Brennagh** the anglicized version of an Irish word meaning 'Welshman'.

Branson, **Branston**, **Bramston** probably a surname given to people who came from a number of places of a similar name – Branston (like the pickles), Brandeston, Brandiston . . . possibly from the Norse name Brand, or from Old English meaning 'firebrand/sword') plus either 'son' or 'stone'.

Brennan, **Brennans**, **Brennand**, **Brennen** possibly from Old English meaning 'burn hand' – a name given to one who carried out punishments (in medieval times). On the other hand, the name could be the anglicization of the Irish name Ó Braonáin ('descendant of Braon', *braon* probably meaning 'grief, sorrow').

Bridge, **Delbridge**, **Dellbridge**, **Dealbridge** from Old English *brycg* meaning a 'dweller near a bridge' or a 'keeper of a bridge';

Bridgeland, **Bridgland** was given as a name to someone who lived on the land near a bridge; **Bridgeman**, **Bridgman** would have been a 'keeper of a bridge', and **Bridger** probably the same, or possibly someone who lived near a bridge. **Brigg**, **Briggs** from Middle English *brigg* also referred to someone living by a bridge. The word 'brigg' for 'bridge' is still used in Scotland today.

Bristow, **Bristowe** from Old English, meaning a 'city situated by a bridge'; the same word as 'Bristol'.

Brock, **Brocks** either from Old French, meaning a 'young stag'; from the Old English, meaning 'badger' (so, as badgers are not noted for their fragrance, probably a nickname arising from the bearer's body odour); or from Old English for 'brook, water meadow', hence 'a dweller by a stream or water meadow'. (*See* **Brook** *below*.)

Brockway from Old English, meaning a 'dweller by a road running by or near a stream'.

Bron *see* Brown.

Brook, **Brooke**, **Brookes**, **Brooking**, **Brooks**, **Broke**, **Bruck** from the Old English meaning 'stream/water meadow', 'brook'), and denoting someone dwelling by a stream.

Brown, **Browne**, **Bron** from Old English, as the name suggests, means the colour brown. The normally pale-skinned English tended to label anyone with a darker skin 'Brown' and over the years the nickname stuck. **Brownson**, **Brunson** probably meant 'son of Brown' rather than 'brown son'.

Brunel *see* **Burnell**

Buchan from Scots Gaelic, meaning either a 'little hut' or more rarely a 'calf'. It is said to be of local origin, given to people from Buchan in Aberdeenshire, but it is also said that the Buchan clan gave their name to the place, so it remains uncertain. The translations from the Gaelic both suggest someone who tended cattle. **Buchan** is the family name of the barons of Tweedsmuir in Scotland.

Bullen, **Bulleyn**, and many variants, probably arise from the English pronunciation of Boulogne and denoted someone who came from the French town.

Bullinger from Old French, meaning a 'baker'.

Buncombe from Old English, meaning 'reed', indicating someone who lived in a 'valley of reeds'.

Bunyan the name of the author of *The Pilgrim's Progress* probably derived from Old French, meaning 'a little swelling, blane' (hence 'bunion'!) and also 'knob, lump' and 'bun, small loaf, patty', so it is likely that the name Bunyan is an occupational one meaning a 'maker of buns and loaves'; although it could have been a nickname for someone disfigured by a lump.

Burger, **Burgess**, **Burgiss**, **Burgh**, **Burke**, along with a number of variants, all come from the Old English, originally meaning 'fort' but coming to mean 'borough'. The names with suffixes like '-er' and '-is(s)' mean 'inhabitant of a borough'. **Burgh** or **Burke** are more likely once to have had the prefix 'de' and would have meant someone coming from a place called Burgh.

Burnell, **Brunel** from an Old French diminutive of 'brown' and most likely to mean someone with a brownish or dark complexion. **Burnet**, **Burnett**, **Burnitt**, derived from another Old French diminutive of 'brown', have the same meaning.

Burnes, **Burness**, **Burns** from Old English, meaning a 'stream' (the word 'burn' is still in use in Scotland today); or it may come from 'burn house' or a place called Burnhouse. The famous Scots poet Robert Burns's original surname was **Burness**, and his family are said to have come from a place called Burnhouse.

The name **Burnside** probably referred to someone who lived by a brook or stream that was long/wide or on a slope by a stream.

Burrel, **Burrell**, **Borrell**, **Borrill** from Old French, meaning a reddish-brown colour and therefore most likely applied to those whose clothing was of this colour or whose complexion was ruddy. Alternatively, it could have referred to the maker of a red-brown woollen cloth called *borel*.

Burton, from Old English, meaning someone who lived in a 'fort enclosure/farm' or, from Middle English, meaning 'manor house', and denoting someone who lived or worked at one.

Butler, **Buttler** from Old French, meaning quite specifically the 'servant in charge of the wine cellar'.

Byers from Old English, meaning someone who worked in a cowshed – a cowhand.

Byfleet from Old English, meaning someone who lived near a 'stream', or who came from a place of that name (located, or once located, by a stream).

Bygrave from Old English, meaning a dweller 'by a trench'; or someone who lived in or by a 'grove'.

Caddell, **Cadel** *see* Caldwell.

Calcraft, **Chalcraft**, **Chalcroft** from the Old English for 'cold', denoting someone who lived in a 'cold croft or cottage'. Similarly, **Caldecot**, **Caldicott**, **Chaldecott** indicated someone who lived in a cold cottage or hut. There are numerous variants of the latter names, including **Calcut**, **Corkitt**, **Colocott** among many others.

Caldwell, **Caddell**, **Cadel**, **Caudwell**, **Chadwell** from Old English meaning a 'cold stream or well', for someone who dwelt near one.

Callaghan from Irish O'Callaghan, meaning 'descendant of Ceallacháin' ('strife').

Callow from Old English, meaning 'bald'.

Cameron when originating in the Highlands, from Scots Gaelic, meaning 'hooked nose', apparently a characteristic of the old clan members. On the other hand, the Lowland Scots so named are almost certainly named after one of three places so called: one near Edinburgh, one in Lennox, and one in Fife.

Campbell from Scots Gaelic, meaning 'crooked mouth' – as with the Highland Camerons a nickname derived from a facial feature – perhaps the original Campbell had a twisted mouth – or perhaps a permanent sneer, or maybe just a wry smile.

Cane, **Kane** from Old French meaning 'cane, reed' – possibly a nickname given to a tall, slim person.

Cannan, **Cannon** from Old Irish, meaning a 'wolf cub'.

Canter, **Kantor** ultimately from the ecclesiastic Latin *cantor* meaning a 'singer'.

Carless from Old English, meaning 'free from worry', probably a nickname given to someone with no worries.

Carnegie from the region of Carnegie in Angus. The original family, called de Balinhard, acquired the land in the fourteenth century and took their name from it. One of the family members, James Carnegie, fifth Earl of Southesk, is the hero of the song 'The Piper o' Dundee', but the most famous person of that name was Andrew Carnegie, who came from a poor and modest background, went to America, and rose to become a multi-millionaire philanthropist.

Carpenter a nickname from the Anglo-French 'carpenter' and referring to anyone who worked with wood.

Carslake, **Caslake Kerslake** from Old English, meaning someone who lived by a 'watercress-stream'. **Carsbrook**, **Caswell**, **Cresswell**, **Kerswill**, and others, all have the same meaning.

Cartwright from Old English, meaning a 'cartmaker'.

Carver from Old English, meaning 'to carve' – it usually referred to someone who worked in wood, sometimes stone.

Casbolt from Middle English, meaning a 'bald-head'.

Catchpole, **Catchpoll** from Old French, meaning 'fowl-chaser' and probably referring to a person authorized to collect poultry in default of money (a kind of taxman); later on, a 'catchpole' came to mean simply a local law-enforcement officer.

Catt, **Chatt** from Old English and Old French for 'cat' and probably first used as a nickname for someone with a cat-like nature.

Caudell, **Caudle** from Medieval Latin, meaning a 'hot, sweet drink'. Usually given to invalids and only very mildly alcoholic, this might have been a nickname for someone who couldn't hold their drink.

Cavel diminutive of Old French, meaning 'bald', a popular nickname.

Cawthorn from Old English, meaning a 'cold, exposed thornbush'. Probably given to someone from one of the places of that name in Yorkshire.

Chaucer from Old French, meaning a maker of shoes, or clothing for the legs, such as hose or breeches.

Challenger a nickname for someone who 'challenges, accuses'.

Chamberlain, **Chamberlaine**, **Chamberlayne**, **Chamberlin** an occupational name meaning an 'attendant to a king or lord'.

Chambers from Old French, meaning a 'room', as a name it probably has much the same meaning as Chamberlain.

Champion from Old French, meaning 'one who fights for a cause'.

Chandler, **Candler** from Old French, meaning a 'candle-maker'.

Chanter from Old French, meaning an 'enchanter, magician', or 'to sing'.

Chaplain, **Chaplin**, **Kaplan** from Old French, meaning a 'priest, clergyman'.

Chapman from Old English, meaning a 'merchant/trader'. The familiar term 'chap' comes from 'chapman'.

Charman from Old French, meaning 'cart' and therefore referring to a 'carter'.

Cheeseman, **Cheasman**, **Cheesman**, **Chisman** from Old English, meaning 'cheese man' – and exactly what it suggests, 'a maker or purveyor of cheese'. **Cheesewright** means, unsurprisingly, someone who makes cheese.

Cheetham, **Cheetam** possibly from Old English meaning either a 'hut on low-lying land near a stream' or 'hut in a village' – but was most likely applied to someone coming from the place of that name in Lancashire.

Cheever, **Chevers** from Old French, meaning 'goat', and therefore referring to someone who was agile – or capricious.

Cheverall, **Cheverell**, **Cheverill** from Old French, meaning 'little goat/kid' and probably referring to a maker or seller of articles made of kid leather; although it might also have been applied as a nickname for a lively, nimble, capering person.

Cheyney, **Cheyne** from Old French, meaning someone who lived next to an 'oak grove'.

Child, **Childe**, **Childs** from Old English, meaning a 'child', one who is immature, or someone who is childish.

Childerhouse, **Childers** from Old English, meaning a 'children's house' or perhaps orphanage.

Chipping from the Old English, meaning a 'market', and referring to someone who lived near or traded at a market. (It is found as part of the name of a number of towns in Great Britain.) The name **Chippendale** probably meant someone who lived in the dale near the market town – somewhat disappointingly as, bearing in mind the famous furniture maker Thomas Chippendale, it would be amusing if it derived from 'chip' as in wood (*see below*).

Chipp, **Chips** might be from Old English, meaning 'price, barter', but is more likely to be a nickname for a carpenter or woodcutter (as in a 'chip' of wood).

Chiswick from Old English, meaning a 'cheese farm'.

Cholmondeley, **Chumley** both pronounced 'Chumley', referring to someone coming from the place in Cheshire. The earliest recorded spelling is 'Chelmundeleg', but its meaning is uncertain.

Christie found especially in Scotland and the North of England, this is very probably a diminutive form of the name 'Christian', and possibly of 'Christopher'.

Chubb from Middle English, meaning the fish. It would have been given as a nickname to someone who resembled the fish either physically – dumpy, chubby – or intellectually – dull-witted.

Churcher, **Churchman**, **Churchouse** for anyone connected with the church, either through employment or from living near one.

Churchill is most likely to mean 'one who lives on a hill by a church', although more fanciful derivations have been suggested, such as 'de Courci'. Winston Churchill is of course the most famous bearer of this name.

Clapp from Old English meaning 'rock' or 'rocky hill', and probably a nickname based on appearance – for someone who was, say, lumpish, like a rock. **Clapton**, meaning 'rocky farm/town', was probably a name given to someone who came from a place of that name.

Clare from the Latin *clara* meaning 'bright, clear'.

Claridge from 'Clarice', a female name that derives from Latin *claritia*, meaning 'brightness'.

Clark, **Clarke**, **Clerk**, **Clerke** from Old English, originally meaning a cleric or clergyman, but coming to mean anyone who was involved with written work. Usually spelled with an *a*, it is one of the commonest British surnames.

Cleave, **Cleaver**, **Cleever** from Old English, meaning to 'cleave or split', it was either someone who split boards for a living, or perhaps chopped down trees. It could also have referred to anyone who lived by a cliff.

Clem, **Clemm**, **Clemans**, **Clemence**, **Clemens**, **Clement**, **Clements** from Latin *Clemens*, meaning either 'mild' or 'merciful'. It was popular as a Christian name in the twelfth century (and the name of several popes), and the surname probably derives from the first name, as do such variants as **Clementson**, **Clemson**, **Climpson**, all meaning 'son of Clement'.

Cliff, **Cliffe**, **Clive**, **Cleave**, **Cleaves**, **Cleef**, **Cleeve**, **Cleeves**, **Cleve**, **Clift**, **Cleft**, like **Cleave** above, from Old English, meaning a 'cliff', 'slope' or 'river bank'. Similarly, **Clifford**, **Clifforth** mean 'someone who lives near a cliff or steep ford'.

Clinton thought to have referred to someone coming from Glinton in Northamptonshire. Whether the place name is from the Middle English *glint* 'slippery' is unclear. Today's most famous bearer of that name, the former President of the United States, Bill Clinton, was in fact born William Jefferson Blythe IV; his father died before he was born; his mother remarried when he was four years old, and when he was fifteen he legally took his stepfather's surname of Clinton.

Coat, Coate, Coates *see* Cote.

Cobbold, Cutbill from Old English, meaning 'famed-bold'.

Cock, Cocks, Cox there are several different meanings attached to this name. It could come from Old Cornish and Welsh *coch*, meaning 'red'; from the Old English *cocc* meaning a 'hillock', but the most likely source is from Old English *cocc* meaning a 'cockerel' and it was probably used as a nickname for particularly feisty young men.

Cody possibly a diminutive of the Middle English *code*, the wax used by cobblers and hence a nickname for a cobbler; alternatively, from the Irish family MacOda from Kilkenny. Buffalo Bill's name was William Frederick Cody

Coe from Old English, meaning 'jackdaw'– perhaps a nickname for a dark-haired or noisy person. If originating in Ireland it might derive from **Coey**, the anglicization of the name Ó Cobhthaigh ('descendant of Cobhthaigh', *cobhthach* meaning 'victorious'). English **Coey**, however, is a variant of **Coy** – meaning exactly that: coy or shy.

Cohen a Hebrew word meaning 'priest'; sometimes, however, it can be a form of the Irish name **Coen** or **Coyne**, the anglicized form of Ó Cadhain ('descendant of Cadhain' *cadhan*, meaning 'wild goose').

Cole, Coles, Colliss from Old English, meaning 'coal' – a nickname for someone with coal-black hair or a dark complexion. **Coleman, Colman** either means someone of a dark complexion, or is an occupational name for a charcoal burner. When of Irish origin, however, the name is probably derived from Ó Colmáin ('descendant of Colmain', originating from *colm*, meaning 'dove').

Colin, Collins, Collen, Collens a diminutive of the name 'Nicholas'.

Colley, Collie from Old English, meaning 'coal-black' – so with the same meaning as **Cole**.

Collier, Colliar, Colyer from Old English meaning 'coal', to denote a 'maker or seller of coal'.

Colt, Coult from Old English, – a nickname bestowed on someone with a lively or frisky nature like a young horse; or a variant of **Coltard, Coltart, Colthard, Colter** meaning a 'keeper of colts'.

Combe, Combes, Coombes, Coombs from Old English, meaning a 'valley' and denoting someone who lived in one.

Conibere, Conibeer, Conybear from Middle English *cony* ('rabbit'- a word still in use), and the Old English word for 'wood' – a name denoting someone who lived in or close to a wood full of rabbits.

Connelly, Connolly from Irish Gaelic, meaning 'conflict' or sometimes 'high-mighty'. The name might also derive from the village Conely in Devon.

Conner from Old English, meaning 'inspector' – not of police, but the person who examined such vital products as ale.

Constable from Old French, meaning an 'officer of the stable'. From there it evolved to mean chief officer of a household, military officer and then parish constable.

Cook, Cooke, Cookes from Old English for 'cook' and probably applied to those who sold cooked meats as well. **Cuxon** is a less obvious variant of **Cookson**, 'son of Cook'.

Cooper, Cowper from Middle English, meaning a 'maker or repairer of wooden buckets'.

Coot, Coote, Coots, Coutts from Middle English, meaning the water bird, the coot, traditionally thought to be stupid, and with a white patch on its head giving the appearance of baldness. It would have been given as a nickname to someone who considered 'daft', or to a bald person.

Cope, **Cape** from Old and Middle English, meaning a 'cape, coat' and probably applied to a 'maker or seller of capes'.

Copeland, **Copland**, **Coupland** from Old Norse, meaning 'bought land'. It was probably given as a surname to people who came from places of such names. The family of the great American composer Aaron Copland, for instance, might well have originated (bearing in mind that spellings changed over the centuries) in Coupland in Cumbria or Coupland in Northumberland.

Copley from Old English, meaning a 'clearing on a hilltop'. A name for someone coming from a place called that or fitting that description.

Corb, **Corbett** from Old French, meaning a 'raven' and possibly denoting someone with very dark hair.

Corey, **Cory**, **Corrie** possibly from Gaelic, meaning a corrie – or circular hollow surrounded by hills, and referring to someone who lives near to one. Spelled with a single *r*, it might derive from a Middle English word meaning a 'shepherd's hut', denoting someone who lived in one.

Cork the Middle English *cork* is a purple-red dye prepared from various lichens, and this would have been given as a name to someone who was either a dyer, or sold or made the dye.

Costain, **Costean**, **Costen** could be a contraction of the name 'Constantine', or of MacAugustin ('son of Augustin').

Costard, **Coster**, **Custer** from Middle English *costard*, a type of apple, later also used to mean 'head'. The word survives in the name of a variety of English apple tree, and in the now rare 'costermonger' – fruit-seller. Another possible derivation for the name, when spelled with a *u* (as in America's George Armstrong Custer of the famed 'Last Stand') is from the Old French for a 'maker of feather-beds'.

Cote, **Cotes**, **Coat**, **Coate**, **Coates** from Old English, meaning a small cottage or hut. There are a number of surnames ending in 'cot', 'cott' or 'cutt' with similar meanings. The name would have been given to someone who lived in one.

Cottel, **Cottell**, **Cottle** from Old French, meaning a 'coat of mail'. But in some cases it might mean a 'short knife' – particularly if spelled **Cuttle**, **Cuttill** (*see also* **Cutler**).

Court, **Courts** from Old French, meaning 'court' or 'manor house', or a similar-sounding word meaning 'short in stature'. So either someone who lived or worked at a large house, or someone small.

Cousen, **Cousin**, **Cozin**, **Cussens** and many other variants from Middle English, meaning a 'kinsman' or 'kinswoman'.

Coward from Old English, meaning a 'cowherd'. Unglamorous, but possibly a relief to some who might have felt the name a slur on some distant ancestor's courage.

Cowdray, **Cowdrey**, **Cowdry** from Old French, meaning 'hazel-copse', denoting someone who lived near a hazel wood.

Crabb, **Crabbe**, **Krabbe** from Old English, meaning 'crab' (a name for someone who walked sideways, perhaps) or from Middle English, meaning the crab apple, a small, sour kind of wild apple and therefore used of people with a sour temperament.

Crabtree from the Middle English (*see above*), denoting someone who lived by 'wild apple trees'.

Craddock from the Welsh name Caradoc (in Latin form Caractacus), meaning 'likeable, amiable'.

Cragg from Gaelic, meaning a 'rock/ crag'.

Crane from Old English, meaning the long-legged bird, and probably describing someone with long, skinny legs like a crane's.

Crawford from Old English, meaning someone dwelling near a 'ford with crows'. Similarly, **Crawley**, **Crowley** would indicate someone who lived in a wood where there were many crows; and **Croyden**, **Croydon** meaning either a 'wood with crows' or a 'valley with crows', the name denoting someone who lived in or by one.

Crease, **Crees**, **Creese** from Old English, meaning 'fine, elegant'.

Creech from Old English, meaning 'creek' – to denote someone who lived by a creek.

Cribb, **Cribbes** from Old English, meaning a 'stall' or 'cattle fold' so probably a name given to someone who tended cattle. The name **Cribbin**, **Cribbins**, however, although it sounds as though it could be a diminutive of Cribbs, has a quite different derivation – it comes from the Irish MacRoibin – 'son of Robin'.

Crier, **Cryer** from Old French, meaning a 'crier', as in town-crier, someone who makes official announcements.

Crisp, **Crispe**, **Cripps** from Old English, meaning 'curly', and so a nickname applied to someone with curly hair.

Crocker, **Croker** from Old English, meaning an 'earthen pot' and probably applied to potters.

Croft, **Crofts**, **Cruft** from Old English, meaning a 'dweller by a croft'.

Cromb, **Crome**, **Croome**, **Crum** from Old English, meaning 'bent', 'crooked' or 'hook', it could be either a nickname for someone who stooped or was hunchbacked, or it could be an occupational name for one who made crooks and staffs. **Crombie**, **Crumbie**, **Crummy** may have the same derivation.

Cromwell originally a place name; from Old English, meaning a 'winding stream'.

Crosby from the Old Norse, meaning a 'farm or village with a cross'.

Cross, **Crosse** from Middle English, meaning a 'cross' and usually denoting someone who dwelt by a village or wayside crucifix. **Crossman** has the same meaning, while **Crossdale** and **Crossley** would have referred to someone who dwelt in, respectively, a valley with a cross and a wood clearing with a cross.

Crouch, **Croucher** from Old English, meaning 'cross' and denoting someone who lived near to one.

[37]

Crowther, Crouther from Middle English, meaning a 'fiddler'.

Cruickshank a Scots name derived from Old Norse, meaning something bent, and Old English 'shanks'. Usually applied to someone who was bowlegged.

Culpepper from 'cull' (in the sense of 'gather') and 'pepper' (to include all spices), meaning a person who dealt in spices.

Culverhouse from Old English, meaning 'dovecote' – to denote the man in charge of a dovecote.

Cuming, Cumings, Cumine, Cummin, Cummins, Cumming, Cummings from the Gaelic, meaning 'bent' or 'crooked'. (*See* **Cameron, Campbell**.)

Currie, Currey, Curry from Scots Gaelic, meaning 'ravine/glen/corrie'.

Curtin a diminutive of Old French for 'short' – a nickname for a short person: 'Shorty'.

Curtis, Curtiss, Curtois from Old French, meaning 'polite', 'courteous', 'of good education' .

Curzon, Curson, Cursons, Corson from Old French, either a diminutive of 'short', or meaning 'a small piece of land'.

Cutler, Cuttler from Old French, meaning a 'cutler' a 'maker or seller of knives'.

Daft from Middle English, meaning 'meek/mild-mannered'.

Dagg from Old French, meaning a 'dagger'.

Dain, **Daine**, **Daines**, **Dayne**, **Daynes** from Old French, meaning someone who is 'worthy/honourable'.

Dalby from Old Norse, meaning a 'valley farm'.

Dale, **Dales** from Old English, meaning a 'dale/valley'.

Dallas from Old English, meaning a dweller at the 'house in the dale/resting place'; there is a Scottish clan of this name.

Dalton from Old English, meaning a 'dale farm'.

Damsell from Old French, meaning a 'maiden' or a 'young squire'.

Dance from Middle English, meaning 'dance' and therefore applied to professional dancers.

Dand, **Dandie**, **Dandy** are all pet forms of the name Andrew.

Dando from Old French, meaning an 'alder grove'.

Dane, **Danes** from Old English, meaning a 'valley'.

Darben from Old English, meaning a 'beloved child'.

Dark, **Darke**, **Darkes** from Old English, meaning 'dark' and applied to those with a swarthy complexion.

Darley from Old English, meaning an 'animal' (most likely a deer).

Darnell from Old English, meaning a 'hidden place'.

Darton from Old English, meaning a 'deer enclosure'.

Dauber, Dawber from Old French, meaning a 'whitewasher'.

David, Davitt from Hebrew *David* meaning 'darling, friend'. **Davey, Davie, Davy** all pet forms of David. **Davidson, Davison, Davisson, Davson, Davies, Davis, Daviss, Davys** all meaning 'son of David'.

Daw, Dawe, Dawes, Daws another diminutive of David, but could also derive from Middle English, meaning a 'jackdaw'.

Dawkins meaning 'Little David'.

Dawlish from Scots Gaelic, for 'black stream'.

Day from Old English, for a 'dairymaid/dairyman'.

Deacon from Old English, for a 'deacon', but ultimately from Greek meaning a 'servant'.

Deal from Old English, meaning a 'valley'.

Dean, Deane, Deanes, Deans, from Middle English, meaning a 'dean'.

Dear, Deare, Deares, Deer, Deere, Deeres from Old English, meaning 'beloved/darling one'.

Death, Deeth, Dearth, D'Eath, D'Eathe from Old English, meaning 'death'.

Debell from Latin, meaning 'weak'.

Deed, Deedes, Dede, Dade from Old English, meaning 'deed'.

Deeping from Old English, meaning a 'deep place'.

Deighton from Old English, meaning a 'place with a ditch around it'.

Delbridge, Dellbridge, Dealbridge *see* **Bridge**.

De la Field, Delafield *see* **Field**.

De la Mare, Delamare, Delamere, Delamore from Old English, meaning 'of the lake/marsh/moor'.

Delf, **Delph**, **Delve**, **Delves** from Old English, meaning a 'dweller by a quarry'.

Dell from Old English, meaning a 'dell'.

Dempsey, **Dempsy** from Irish, meaning 'proud'.

Dempster from Old English, meaning a 'judge'.

Dence, **Dench** from Middle English, meaning 'Danish'.

Denholm, **Denholme** from Old English, meaning a 'dweller by the house'. Also the name of several localities in Scotland.

Denis, **Denise**, **Dennis**, **Denniss**, **Dennys** the name of several saints, and also from Old French, meaning 'Danish'.

Denison, **Dennison**, either 'son of Den(n)is', or from Old French, meaning 'someone living in a city and enjoying all the privileges that come with that' ('denizen').

Denleigh, **Denley**, **Denly** from Old English, meaning a 'dweller by a clearing in a valley'.

Denmar from Old English, meaning a 'maker of dams'.

Devenish, **Devonish** from Old English, meaning a 'man from Devon'.

Deveraux, **Devereaux** probably from the Celtic, meaning 'dwellers by the Ebura river'. That is, the Eure River in Normandy.

Devin, **Devine**, **Devinn** from Middle English, meaning 'divine'.

Dewar from Scots Gaelic, meaning a 'pilgrim'.

Dewhurst from Old English, meaning a 'damp wood/forest'.

Dibble a diminutive form of 'Theobald'.

Dibden, **Dibdin** from Old English, meaning a 'deep valley/gorge'.

Dick, **Dicken**, **Dickens**, **Dickins**, **Dickie** (Scots), diminutive forms of 'Richard'.

Dickenson, **Dickinson**, **Dickerson**, **Dickson**, **Dixon** all meaning 'son of Richard'.

Difford from Old English, meaning a 'deep ford'.

Digg, **Digges** from Middle English, meaning a 'duck' and probably first used as a nickname.

Diggatt from Old French, meaning a 'maker of spurs'.

Dilworth from Old English, for a 'place where dill grows'.

Dimblebee, **Dimbleby** from Old Norse, meaning a 'gorge'.

Dingle from Old English, meaning a 'dell/hollow'.

Dinmore from Old Welsh, meaning a 'large hill'.

Diplock from Old English, meaning a 'deep stream'.

Ditchett from Old English, meaning a 'gate in the dike'.

Dobb, **Dobbe**, **Dobbie**, **Dobbs** all diminutives of the name 'Robert', from which come such names as **Dobbin** or **Dobson**.

Dod, **Dodd**, **Dodds**, **Dods** from Old German, meaning something that is 'rounded/lumpish' and therefore a nickname for a 'lumpish man' or someone stupid.

Donald from Scots Gaelic, for 'world mighty'. **MacDonald** – 'son of Donald'.

Donat from Latin *donatus* meaning 'given'.

Donnelly Irish, from O'Donnelly 'descendant of Brown Valour'.

Donovan Irish, from O'Donovan 'descendant of Dark Brown'.

Doolan Irish, from O'Dooley 'descendant of Black Defiance'.

Dooley Irish, from O'Dooley 'descendant of Black Hero'.

Dormer from Old French, meaning a 'sleeper' and therefore applied to lazy people.

Dottrell from Middle English, denoting a species of plover, considered a 'dotty' bird and often applied to foolish people.

Doublet, **Doublett** from Old French, meaning a 'doublet' and applied to a 'maker of doublets'.

Douce, **Dowse**, **Duce** from Middle English, meaning 'sweet'. **Dowsett** a diminutive of Dowse.

Dougal, **Dougall** from Old Gaelic and Irish, meaning a 'black stranger'.

Dove from Old English, meaning a 'dove' and denoting gentleness.

Dow from Scots Gaelic, for 'black'.

Dowd Irish, from O'Dowd 'descendant of Black'.

Down, **Downe** from Old English, meaning a 'down or hill'.

Downham from Old English, meaning a 'home on the hill'.

Downing from Old English, meaning 'of the family of Down/ Dunn'.

Drabble from Scots Gaelic, meaning 'dirty'.

Drake from Old English, meaning a 'dragon'.

Draper, **Drapper** from Old French, meaning a 'maker or seller of cloth'.

Drawer from Old English, meaning 'carrier/transporter'.

Dray from Old English, meaning a 'sledge/dray'.

Draycott from Old English, meaning a 'place for keeping sledges'.

Drayton from Old English, meaning a 'steep sledge track'.

Drew there are various meanings for this name. In Old English, it meant a 'ghost, phantom', but Drew is also a diminutive of 'Andrew', so it might come from that. Alternatively, in Old French it meant 'sturdy'.

Drewery, **Drewry**, **Drury** from Old French, meaning 'love/love-token'.

Dringer from Old English, meaning a 'drinker'.

Drinkwater from Old English, meaning quite literally 'drink water' and probably applied to a very poor person, that is, someone who could not afford to buy ale.

Driver from Old English, meaning a 'driver of animals'.

Drummond from Scots Gaelic, meaning a 'ridge'.

Dubois from Old French, meaning 'from the wood'.

Ducker from Old English, meaning 'someone who bred or hunted ducks'. A 'ducker' was also a fighting-cock and so the name might well be a nickname for someone with an aggressive nature.

Duckham from Old English, meaning a 'river meadow'.

Duckworth from Old English, meaning an 'enclosure with ducks'.

Duff from both Irish and Scots Gaelic, meaning 'black' and applied to those with a dark complexion.

Duffield from Old English, meaning a 'field with doves'.

Dulwich from Old English, meaning a 'meadow where dill is grown'.

Duncan from Gaelic, meaning a 'brown warrior'.

Dunham from Old English, meaning a 'hill farm'.

Dunn, **Dunne**, **Duns** from Old English, meaning 'dark, black, brown, swarthy'. 'Dunce' derives from the fourteenth-century scholar John Duns Scotus, whose followers were ridiculed in the sixteenth century as fools and dullards.

Dunstan, **Dunston** from Old English, meaning a 'hill stone'.

Dupont from Old French, meaning 'of the bridge'.

Durham from Old Norse, and Old English, meaning a 'hill peninsula'.

Durnford from Old English, meaning a 'hidden ford'.

Dyke from Old English, meaning a 'ditch'.

Dymock from Old Welsh meaning a 'pigsty'.

Ead, Eade, Eades, Eads from Old English, meaning 'happiness'.

Eam, Eame, Eams, Eames from Old English, meaning a 'son of the uncle'.

Eardley from Old English, meaning a 'dwelling place in a clearing'.

Earl, Earle from Old English, meaning an 'earl' and applied either to one of high rank or to someone who appeared of high rank.

Earley from Old English, meaning a 'ploughed field'.

Earnshaw from Old English, meaning a 'dweller by an eagle wood'.

Earp from Old English, meaning 'swarthy' – a nickname arising from someone's complexion.

East, Eastes, Este from Old English, meaning a 'man from the east'. **Eastbrook, Eastabrook, Easterbrook** therefore denoted someone who dwelt 'east of the brook'; **Easterby** someone who 'lived east of the village'; **Eastwood** someone who 'lived east of a wood' or 'eastward', and **Escott** someone from 'the eastern cottage' or 'east of the cottage'.

Eastman, Esmond, Esmonde from Old English, meaning 'grace'.

Eccles from Old Welsh, meaning a 'church', and **Ecclestone** a 'church farm'.

Edgar from Old English, meaning a 'prosperity spear'.

Edge from Old English, meaning someone who lived 'near a prominent ridge'.

Edington from Old English, meaning a 'wasteland hill'.

Edmund from Old English, meaning 'prosperity protector'.

Edward, **Edwarde**, **Edwardes**, **Edwards** from Old English, meaning a 'prosperity guardian'.

Elder, **Elders** from Old English, meaning the 'elder/senior' one.

Elgar, **Elphick**, **Alphege** from Old English, meaning 'elf/fairy high'.

Elvey from Old English, meaning an 'elf gift'. **Elward** from Old English, meaning an 'elf protector'. **Elwood** from Old English, meaning an 'elf ruler'.

Elinson meaning 'son of Helen'.

Eliot, **Eliott**, **Elliot**, **Elliott** from Old English, meaning an 'elf ruler'.

Ellen, **Ellens**, **Ellin**, **Ellins**, **Elen**, **Elens**, **Hellen**, **Hellens** Greek for 'the bright one' but more likely from Old English, meaning a 'dweller by the alders'.

Elliman, **Ellerman**, **Elman** from Old English, meaning 'oil man' – a 'seller of oil'.

Elm from Old English, denoting someone who lived by elm trees, or an elm tree. **Elmore** for someone living on a 'moor with elms'.

Elwes from Old German, meaning 'wide'.

Ely from Old English, meaning an 'eel place'.

Endacott, **Endicott** from Old English, meaning 'place beyond the cottages'.

Enfield from Old English, meaning a 'place beyond the field'.

Enright, from MacEnright, 'son of Ionnrachtaigh'; its meaning is uncertain – scholars have suggested the name is from *inreachtach*, meaning 'lawful', but others say it is from *indreacht*, meaning 'attack' (and if the *in* of *inreachtach* were to be seen as a negative rather than an intensive prefix, the word would mean 'unlawful'!).

Erwin, **Everwin**, **Irwin**, **Irwine**, **Irwing**, **Urwin** from Old English, meaning 'friend of the boar' and probably denoting someone who bred or looked after them.

Etheredge, **Etheridge** from Old English, meaning of 'noble rule'.

Eustace, **Eustice**, **Eustis** from Greek, meaning 'fruitful'.

Evans the Welsh form of 'John'.

Everard, **Everatt** from Old German, meaning 'boar hard'.

Ewan, **Ewen**, **Ewens**, **Ewing**, **Ewings** ultimately from Greek, meaning someone who was 'well born'.

Ewbank, **Ewbanks**, **Ubank** from Old English, meaning someone who lives by a 'yew bank'.

Ewer, **Ewers** from Old French, and referring to a 'servant who supplied water to a host's guests'.

Eye from Old English, meaning a resident of a 'low-lying land' or an 'island'.

Eyton from Old English, referring to a general 'place on a river'.

Faber from Latin *faber* meaning a 'smith' and usually referring to someone's occupation.

Fabian the most likely source for this name is from Latin *faba* meaning a 'bean' and perhaps referring to someone who grew, bought or sold beans.

Fage from Middle English, meaning 'deceit'.

Fagg, **Fagge** from Old English, meaning 'clean bread' and therefore given to bakers.

Faggeter from Middle English, meaning a 'bundle of sticks' and therefore used for a 'maker of faggots'.

Fair, **Faire**, **Faires**, **Fairs** from Old English, meaning 'fair/ beautiful'. Similar 'fair' names include **Fairbairn**, **Fairbairns**, **Fairbarns** and, **Fairchild** meaning a 'beautiful child'; **Fairbank**, **Fairbanks** denoting a 'dweller by the fair bank'; **Fairhead** for someone thought to have a 'fair/handsome head'; **Fairlee** for someone living by a 'beautiful woodland clearing'; **Fairman**, **Fayerman**, **Fierman**, **Fireman** meaning a 'fair-headed/handsome man', and **Fairwell**, **Farewell** for someone living close to a 'beautiful spring'.

Fairbrass from Old French, meaning a 'fierce/strong arm'.

Fairley from Old English, meaning a 'clearing of ferns'.

Fairweather from Middle English, denoting someone with a 'sunny disposition'.

Falconer, Falconar, Falkner, Faulkner from Old French, meaning a person 'who hunts with hawks'.

Falk, Fawke, Fawkes, Falk, Faulkes, Faulks all from Old French/Old German, meaning a 'falcon' and probably referring to someone who kept or worked with these birds.

Fall, Falle, Falls from Middle English, meaning 'someone who lives by a fall/waterfall'.

Fallow, Fallows from Old English, meaning someone who lives 'by newly ploughed/cultivated land'.

Fane, Fayne, Faynes from Old English, and Middle English, meaning 'well disposed'.

Fann, Van, Vann from Old English, meaning a 'fen', and so denoting the same as **Fanner, Vanner** – a 'dweller by a fen'.

Faringdon from Old English, meaning a 'hill of bracken'.

Farley probably from Middle English, 'fern leigh', meaning a 'meadow or clearing with ferns'.

Farmer from Old French, meaning 'a person who collects taxes/a bailiff'.

Farnfield from Old English, meaning 'someone who dwells by land covered with ferns'.

Farquhar, Farquar from Gaelic, meaning 'dear one'.

Farrar, Farrer, Farrah these are all variations of the name **Ferrer**.

Farson meaning a 'fair son'.

Faulkner *see* **Falconer**.

Faun, Faunce, Fawn from Middle English, meaning 'a young deer' and probably used to denote someone with a lively nature.

Favel, Favell, Favelle from Old French, meaning 'tawny coloured' and probably alluding to hair colour.

Fay, Faye from Old French, meaning a 'fairy'.

Fear, **Feare** from Middle English, meaning a 'comrade'.

Fearnside from Old English, meaning 'someone who lives on a ferny hill'.

Feather from Old English, meaning a 'feather' and denoting either a buyer or seller of feathers.

Fell from Old Norse, meaning a 'fell/mountain' or from Old English, meaning an 'animal skin'.

Fellow, **Fellowe**, **Fellows**, **Fellowes** from Old Norse, meaning a 'companion'.

Felton from Old English, meaning a 'dwelling in a field'.

Fenn, **Venn** from Old English, a 'fen/marsh', so having the same meaning as **Fenner** – 'someone who lives by a fen'.

Fenwick from Old English, meaning 'a dairy farm in a fen'.

Fergus from Old Irish, meaning 'man choice'.

Fern, **Ferne**, **Ferns**, **Fearn**, **Fearne** from Old English, meaning 'someone who lived in/near ferns'.

Ferrer, **Ferrar**, **Farrer** from Old French, meaning a 'worker in iron'.

Ferret from Old French, meaning a 'ferret'.

Ferry, **Ferrie**, **Ferrey** from Middle English, a 'ferry', the same name as **Ferriman**, **Ferryman**, meaning 'someone who works a ferry'.

Fetters from Middle English, meaning 'someone who makes things'.

Feverel from Old English, meaning 'February'.

Fewster from Old French, meaning 'someone who makes saddle trees'.

Fidler, **Fiddler**, **Vidler** from Old English, meaning 'someone who plays the fiddle'.

Field, **Fields**, **de la Field**, **Delafield** from Old English, meaning a 'field' and denoting someone who lived on or by cultivated land.

Fielder from Old English, meaning someone who worked 'in the fields'.

Fielding from Old English, meaning someone who lived 'in the countryside'.

Figgess, **Figgis** from Old French, meaning 'faithful'.

Fill, **Fills**, **Filson** a diminutive of 'Philip'.

Finch from Old English, meaning a 'finch' and perhaps applied to someone of little intelligence i.e. a 'bird brain'.

Findlay, **Findley**, **Finlay**, **Finley** from Scots Gaelic, meaning a 'fair hero'.

Fine, **Fines** from Old French, meaning 'delicate'.

Finn, **Fynn** from Irish Gaelic, meaning 'descendant of Fionn' (*fionn* means 'fair').

Firebrace from Middle English, meaning 'bold/fierce'.

Firth, **Frith** from Old English, meaning a 'woodland'.

Fishbourne, **Fishburn**, **Fishburne** from Old English, meaning a 'stream with fish'.

Fisher from Old English, meaning a 'fisherman'.

Fishwick from Old English, meaning a 'dairy farm where fish was sold'.

Fitz a prefix from Anglo-French *fiz* meaning 'son of'.

Flash, **Flasher**, **Flashman** from Middle English, meaning a 'pond' or 'person who lives by a pond'.

Fleet from Old English, meaning 'someone who lives by a stream.'

Fleming, **Flemming** from Old French, meaning 'a man who comes from Flanders'.

Flesher from Old English, denoting 'flesh' and probably denoting someone who 'cut up meat' i.e. a butcher.

Fletcher from Old French, meaning a 'maker of arrows'.

Fleury, **Florey**, **Flory** from Latin *flos* meaning a 'flower'.

Flitter from Old English, meaning 'someone who disputes things'.

Floater a derivative from the Old English word for 'ship' and therefore meaning a 'sailor'.

Flower, **Flowers** from Old English, meaning an 'arrow' and therefore applied to a 'maker of arrows'.

Flutter from Middle English, meaning a person 'who plays flute'.

Fodor from Middle English, meaning 'feed' and applied to those who 'fed livestock'.

Fold, **Foldes**, **Folds** from Old English, meaning 'someone who worked in a cattle pen'.

Follet, **Follett**, **Folley**, **Folly** from Old French, meaning 'foolish'.

Foot, **Foote** from Old English, meaning 'foot'.

Footman from Old English, probably referring to a 'foot soldier'.

Forbes probably Scots Gaelic, for a 'field'.

Ford, **Forde**, **Forth** from Old English, meaning 'someone who lives by a ford'.

Foreman, **Forman**, **Forward**, **Forwood** from Old English, meaning a 'swineherd'.

Forester, **Forestier**, **Forrester**, **Forrestor** from Middle English, meaning 'someone in charge of the forest'.

Forge from Old English, meaning a 'blacksmith'.

Foss, **Voss** from Old English, meaning a 'ditch'. There was also a Roman roadway called the Fosse Way.

Foster there are two different meanings to this word: from Old French, the meaning applies to a 'maker of scissors/shears' but from Old English, the meaning applies to a 'foster-parent/child'.

Fower from Old French, meaning a 'hearth-keeper'.

Fowle, Fowles, Fowell, Fowells, Fowls from Old English, meaning a 'bird' and probably applied to a keeper of birds.

Foyle from Old English, meaning 'someone who lived by a pit'.

Frain, Frane, Frayn, Frayne from Old French, meaning a 'dweller by an ash tree'.

Frances, Francis, Franses from French, meaning a 'Frenchman'.

Frankham, Frankhom, Frankcombe, Francom, Francomb, Francombe from Old French, meaning 'free'.

Franklin, Franklyn, Franklen from Middle English, meaning a 'landowner of free but not of noble birth'.

Frater from Old French, meaning someone 'in charge of a refectory'.

Frear, Freer, Friar, Frier, Fryer from Old French, meaning a 'friar'.

Frederick, Fredericks from Old German, meaning 'peace rule'.

Freebody from Old English, meaning a 'freeman'.

Freemantle from Old French, meaning 'poorly dressed'.

Freshwater from Old English, meaning 'freshwater' and applied to someone who sold water.

Frobisher, Furber, Forber from Old French, meaning a 'polisher, or furbisher, of swords and armour'.

Frome from Old Welsh, probably meaning 'fine'.

Frost from Old English, meaning 'frost' and most likely applied to people with white/grey hair.

Froud, Froude, Frowd from Old English, meaning 'prudent'.

Fry, Frye from Old English, meaning 'free'.

Fuller, Voller, Vollers from Old English, and Old French, meaning a 'scourer (fuller) of cloth'.

Fullshawe, Fullwood from Old English, meaning 'someone who lives by a muddy forest/wood'.

Furlong, Furlonge from Old English, meaning 'one furrow long'.

Furnell from Old French, meaning a 'furnace'.

Furner, Fournier from Old French, meaning a 'baker'.

Furr from Middle English, meaning 'a coat of fur'.

Furse, Furze, Furseman, Furzeman, Furzer, Fursey, Fussey from Old English, meaning 'someone who lives among/near furze bushes'.

Gabb from Old French, meaning 'deceiver/liar'.

Gabriel from Hebrew, meaning 'God is a strong man'.

Gage from Old Norse and Old French, meaning someone who 'measures'.

Gain, **Gaine**, **Gaines** from Old French, meaning 'someone who is tricky'.

Gainford from Old English, meaning a 'direct ford'.

Gait, **Gaite**, **Gaites**, **Gaitt** from Old French, meaning a 'watchman'.

Galbraith, **Galbreath** from Scots Gaelic, meaning a 'stranger Briton', i.e. those people who had settled in Scotland but weren't born there.

Gale, **Gayle** there are two very different meanings to this name. The first is from Old English, and means 'light, merry, joyous', while the second is from Middle English, and means 'jail/jailer'. Similarly, **Gayler** or **Gaylor** means 'jailer'.

Galley, **Gally**, **Galey** from Middle English, meaning a 'galley' and referring to a 'galleyman/rower'.

Galliard, **Gaillard**, **Gallard** from Old French, meaning 'full of spirits'.

Galpin, **Galpen** from Old French, meaning 'to gallop' and thus applied to messengers.

Galsworthy from Old English, meaning 'dweller by a windswept slope'.

Gambell, **Gambel**, **Gammell**, **Gammil** from Old Norse, meaning 'old'.

Gant *see* **Gaunt**.

Ganter an occupational name from the French *gantier* meaning 'someone who makes gloves'.

Gape, **Gapes** from Old French, meaning 'weak'.

Gard, **Guard** from Old French, meaning a 'guard/watchman'.

Garland from Old French, meaning a 'garland' and probably denoting someone who made and or sold them.

Garlic, **Garlick**, **Garlicke** from Old English, meaning 'garlic' and probably referring to someone who sold it.

Garner, **Garnar** from Old French, meaning a 'keeper of the granary'.

Garnon from Old French, meaning 'moustache'. (Moustaches weren't common amongst the clean-shaven Normans.)

Garrad, **Garrett**, **Garritt**, **Garrod** from the name 'Gerald'. **Garrettson**, **Garrison** etc meaning a 'son of Gerald'.

Garth from Old Norse, meaning 'an enclosure'.

Garston, **Garstone** from Old English, meaning 'someone who lived by a fenced-off farm'.

Gatcomb, **Gatcombe** from Old English, meaning a 'field of goats', while **Gatland** means 'goat-land' – denoting people who lived in or by such a place. (*See also* **Gotham**.)

Gate, **Gates** from Old English, meaning a 'gate' and therefore applied to gate-keepers.

Gatherer from Old English, meaning a 'gatherer' and most likely applied to tax-collectors.

Gaunt, **Gant** from Middle English, meaning either 'slim' or 'haggard-looking'.

Gaylord from Old French, meaning someone with 'high spirits'.

Gear from Old Norse, meaning an 'impulse/fad'.

Geddes from Scots Gaelic, meaning a 'ridge'.

Geldard, **Geldart**, **Gelder** from Old English, meaning a 'one who tends cattle', or from Middle English, meaning 'barren'.

Gelder *see* **Gilder**.

Gerald, **Jarrod** from Old German, meaning 'spear brave/ruler'.

Gervase from Old German, meaning a 'spear servant'.

Gething, **Gettings**, **Gitting**, **Gittings** from Old Welsh, meaning someone of swarthy complexion.

Gibben, **Gibbens**, **Gibbin**, **Gibbins**, **Gibbings**, **Gibbon**, **Gibbons** from Old German, meaning a 'gift friend'.

Giffard, **Gifford** from Old French, meaning 'bloated'.

Gilbert from Old German, meaning 'hostage bright'.

Gilchrest, **Gilchrist** from Irish/Scots Gaelic, meaning a 'servant of Christ'.

Gilder, **Gilders**, **Gelder** from Old English, meaning 'to gild' and applied to people who gilded as a profession.

Gildon from Old English, meaning 'golden'.

Gill from Scots Gaelic, meaning a 'servant'.

Gillespey, **Gillespie** from Scots Gaelic, meaning a 'bishop's servant'.

Gillibrand from Old German, meaning a 'hostage sword'.

Gillingham from Old English, meaning the 'homestead of Gylla's followers'.

Gilly from Old Cornish, meaning 'someone who lives by a grove'.

Gilmour, **Gilmore** from Irish Gaelic, meaning 'servant of the Virgin Mary'.

Ginger from Middle English, meaning 'ginger' and either applied to someone who grew/sold ginger or who was red-haired/hot-headed.

Girdler from Old English, meaning a 'maker of girdles'.

Girle from Middle English, meaning a 'youth/maiden'.

Gladden, **Gladding**, **Glading** from Old English, meaning 'glad'.

Glade from Old English, meaning a 'dweller in or by a glade'.

Glaisher, **Glazier** from Old English, meaning 'glass-maker'.

Glazebrook from Old English, meaning a 'blue stream'.

Gleave from Old French, meaning a 'sword'.

Glover from Old English, meaning a 'maker or seller of gloves'.

Goacher from Old English, meaning 'cheerful face'.

Godbear, **Godbeer**, **Godber** from Old English, meaning 'May God be here/in this house'.

Godfrey from Old German, meaning 'God peace'.

Godrich, **Godridge** from Old English, meaning a 'god ruler/a benign ruler'.

Godsal, **Godsall** from Old French, meaning a 'good soul'.

Godwin, **Godwyn**, **Goodwin**, **Goodwyn** from Old English, meaning a 'god protector/friend'.

Gold, **Gould**, **Golden** from Old English, meaning 'gold/golden-haired'.

Goldburg, **Goldburgh** from Old English, meaning a 'gold fort'.

Goldrich from Old English, meaning 'gold ruler'.

Goldway from Old English, meaning a 'gold warrior'.

Golightly from Old English, meaning 'swift of foot' and probably applied to a messenger.

Gomer from Old English, meaning a 'good battle'.

Gooch, **Goodge**, **Goudge**, **Gough** from Welsh, meaning 'red' and probably referring to a red-faced or red-haired man.

Gooday, **Goodey** from Old English, meaning an 'occupant of the good enclosure'.

Goodbairn, **Goodchild** from Middle English, meaning 'good child'. Other 'Good' names include **Goodbody** meaning a 'good/healthy body'; **Goodfellow** a 'good man/friend/associate'; **Goodhew** a 'good heart/mind'; **Goodison** from Old English, meaning a 'son of God'; **Goodley** denoting someone who lived in or near a 'good woodland clearing', and **Goodyear** meaning a 'good year'.

Goosey from Old English, meaning 'an island of geese'.

Gordon from Scots Gaelic, for a 'great hill'.

Gore from Old English, for a 'plot of ground that is spear-shaped'; similarly, **Gorham** means a 'spear-shaped meadow', both names denoting someone who lived on or by such a piece of land.

Gosford from Old English, meaning a 'goose crossing/ford'.

Goslin, **Gosling** from Middle English, meaning a 'gosling'.

Goss, **Gosse** a diminutive form of 'Jocelyn' or 'Gosling'.

Gossard from Old English, meaning a 'goose herd'.

Gotham from Old English, meaning a 'homestead with goats'.

Gourd from Old French, meaning something or someone who is 'course/unrefined/lumpy'.

Gover from Middle English, meaning 'gently, beautifully'.

Gower, **Gowar**, **Gowers**, from Old German, meaning 'good army'.

Grace, **Gracey** from Old French, meaning 'grey'.

Grafton from Old English, meaning a 'farm by a grove'.

Grand from Old French, meaning 'big, tall' or 'old, senior'.

Gratton from Old English, meaning a 'large hill'.

Grave, **Graves** from Middle English, meaning a 'steward' or 'someone in charge' (most likely of property).

Graveney from Old English, meaning a 'stream in the trench'.

Grayrigge from Old Norse, meaning a 'grey ridge'.

Grealey from Old French, meaning 'marked by hailstones' but probably referring to the condition of a person's skin, most likely that it was pock-marked.

Greave, **Greaves** from Old English, meaning a 'grove'.

Greener from Old English, meaning a 'dweller by a green bank'. Other 'Greens' include **Greenham** for someone living by a 'green water meadow'; **Greenhead** for one who habitually wore a green hood; **Greensmith** meaning someone 'who works with copper', and **Greenwood** for one who dwelt in or next to a green wood.

Greer a diminutive form of the name 'Gregory'.

Greet from Old English, meaning 'gravel'.

Grieg diminutive Scots form of the name 'Gregory' (from the Greek for 'watchful').

Grew, **Grewe** from Old French, for a 'crane'.

Grewal from Old French, meaning 'flour/meal' and probably applied to a baker or miller.

Grice, **Grise**, **Griss** there are two different meanings to this name: it could come from Old Norse, meaning a 'pig', or from Old French, meaning 'grey-haired'.

Grierson meaning 'son of Gregor'.

Grieve, **Grieves** from Old English, meaning a 'governor/overseer'.

Griffith, **Griffiths** from Welsh, meaning 'lord/chief'.

Grigg, **Griggs** a diminutive form of the name 'Gregory'.

Grill, **Grills**, **Grylls** from Old English, meaning 'gnashing of teeth/rage/ wrath'.

Grimble, **Grumble** most likely from Old German, meaning 'helmet bold'.

Grime, Grimes, Grimm, Grimme from Old English, meaning 'fierce'.

Grimstead, Grimsteed from Old English, meaning a 'green homestead'.

Grindal, Grindell, Grindle from Old English, meaning a 'green hill'.

Griswold from Old English, meaning 'somewhere with pebbles'.

Groom from Middle English, meaning a 'servant, farm-worker'.

Gross from Latin meaning 'thick' and from Old French, meaning 'fat'.

Grosser from Old French, meaning 'someone who dealt in wholesale goods'.

Grosvenor from Old French, meaning a 'chief huntsman'.

Grove, Groves from Old English, meaning 'someone who lives by a grove'.

Grubb, Grubbe from Middle English, meaning a 'grub' and applied to someone of small stature.

Gubell from Old English, meaning 'battle bold'.

Gudgeon from Old French, meaning 'greedy'.

Gull from Middle English, meaning either 'gull' or 'pale'.

Gulliver from Old French, meaning a 'glutton'.

Gumbold of German origin, meaning 'battle bold'.

Gunn from Old Norse, meaning 'war/battle'.

Guthrie from Scots Gaelic, meaning 'windswept'.

Guyat *see* **Wyatt**.

Guyer, Gyer from Old French, meaning a 'guide'.

Gwyn, Gwynn, Gwynne from Old Welsh meaning 'white', for someone with white hair or a white face.

Habbeshaw, **Habeshaw** from Old French, meaning 'a maker of coats of mail'.

Hacker from Middle English, meaning 'someone who cuts/hacks' probably wood.

Hadley, **Hadlee** from Old English, meaning a 'clearing/field' and referring to someone who lived close to one.

Haggard, **Haggart**, **Hagard** from Old French, meaning 'untamed'.

Haig, **Haigh**, **Hague** from Old English, and Old Norse, meaning 'someone who lives by an enclosure'.

Hailey, **Hayley** from Old English, meaning a 'dweller by a hay clearing'.

Haim, **Haimes**, **Haymes** from Old German, meaning 'home'.

Hain, **Haine**, **Heyne** from Old English, meaning a 'fenced-off area'; or possibly from Old Norse, meaning someone who is 'niggardly'.

Haldane, **Halden**, **Holdane** from Old Norse, meaning 'half-Dane', a nickname for a person who was half Danish.

Halford from Old English, denoting someone dwelling near a ford by a 'haugh', or low-lying riverside meadow.

Halifax from Old English, meaning a 'holy field'.

Haliwell from Old English, meaning a 'holy well/spring'.

Hall, **Halle**, **Halls** from Old English, meaning someone dwelling or employed at a 'hall/manor house'.

Hallam from Old English, meaning 'at the rocks'.

Hallman, **Halman** from Old English, meaning a 'servant at the hall/manor house'.

Hallmark *see* **Allmark**.

Halloway *see* **Alaway**.

Hallowes, **Hallows** from Old English, meaning a 'dweller in the valley'.

Ham, **Hamm**, **Hamme**, **Hams** from Old English, meaning 'someone who lives by a stream'.

Hampden from Old English, meaning a 'homestead valley'.

Hamper from Old French, meaning a 'seller of goblets'.

Hanbury from Old English, meaning a 'fort/manor house'.

Hand, **Hands** from Old English, meaning 'hand' and possibly denoting someone who was good at making things with their hands.

Hansard from Old French, meaning a 'cutlass'.

Hansell *see* **Ansell**.

Harberer, **Harbisher** from Old English, meaning a 'lodge-house keeper'.

Harbourn, **Harbourne** from Old English, meaning a 'dirty/polluted stream'.

Harcourt from Old English, meaning a 'falconer's cottage'.

Hardcastle from Old English, meaning a 'cheerless dwelling place'.

Harden from Old English, meaning 'grey'.

Harding from Old English, meaning a 'hard man/warrior'.

Hardwick from Old English, meaning a 'cattle/sheep farm'.

Hardy, **Hardey**, **Hardie** from Middle English, meaning bold/brave'.

Hare, **Hares** from Old English, meaning a 'hare' and probably used to denote 'speed'.

Harker from Middle English 'hark, hearken', meaning 'to listen' and therefore applied to eavesdroppers and spies.

Harland from Old English, meaning 'someone who lives by the edge of a wood'.

Harlock, **Horlock**, **Horlick** from Old English, meaning 'grey hair'.

Harman, **Harmand**, **Harmon**, **Harmond** from Old German, meaning a 'warrior'.

Harper from Old English, meaning a 'maker of harps'.

Harrington from Old English, meaning a 'family farm'.

Harrop from Old English, meaning a 'hares' valley'.

Hart from Old English, meaning a 'deer', for someone who resembled one or one who hunted deer. **Hartfield**, meaning a 'field with deer', **Hartford**, meaning a 'ford used by deer', and **Hartley**, meaning a 'deer wood', would have been given as names to people who dwelt in or near such landmarks.

Harwich from Old English, meaning an 'army camp'.

Haslam from Old English, meaning 'dweller by the hazels'.

Hatch, **Hatcher** from Old English, meaning someone who 'lives by the gate'.

Hathaway, **Hathway** from Old English, meaning a 'war warrior'.

Hatt, **Hatts** from Old English, meaning a 'dweller by the hill'.

Havelock from Old Norse, meaning 'sea port'.

Haw, **Hawes** from Old English, meaning 'someone who lives by the enclosure'.

Haward from Old Norse, meaning 'chief warden/keeper'.

Hawk, **Hawke**, **Hawker**, **Hawkes**, **Hawks** from Old English, meaning 'hawk' and most probably applied to a keeper of hawks, a falconer.

Hawthorn, **Hawthorne** from Old English, meaning 'someone who lives near hawthorns'.

Hawtin from Old French, meaning 'proud, haughty'.

Hay, **Haye**, **Hayes**, **Hays**, **Hey**, **Heye**, **Heyes** from Old English, meaning 'a fenced-off area' (sometimes for hunting).

Hayton from Old English, meaning a 'hay farm'.

Hayward from Old English, meaning a 'guardian of a fenced-off enclosure/field'.

Hazelwood, **Aizlewood** from Old English, meaning a 'hazel wood' and referring to someone who lived close to one.

Head from Old English, meaning 'top of a hill/valley'.

Heal, **Heale**, **Heals**, **Heales** from Middle English, meaning a 'dweller in a secluded place'.

Hearn, **Hearne** *see* **Hern**.

Heath from Old English, for someone who lived on or close to an area of heathland. Likewise, **Heathcote**, a 'cottage on a heath' and **Heathfield**, a 'heather-filled field'.

Hebdon from Old English, meaning a 'valley where there are hips growing'.

Hellen, **Hellens** *see* **Ellen**.

Helliar, **Hellier**, **Hellyer**, **Helyer**, **Hilliar**, **Hillier** from Old English, meaning a 'roof tiler' (to 'hill' something used to mean 'to cover' it).

Hempstead from Old English, meaning a 'homestead'.

Hems from Old English, meaning 'someone who lives by the border'.

Henderson meaning 'son of Henry'.

Hendy from Middle English, meaning 'kind/courteous'.

Herald, **Heraud**, **Herold**, **Herod** from Middle English, meaning a 'herald'.

Herbert from Old German, meaning 'army bright'.

Herd, **Heard**, **Hird**, **Hurd**, **Herdman** from Old English, meaning a 'herd, herdsman'.

Here from Middle English, meaning 'gentle/kind'.

Hern, **Herne**, **Hearn**, **Hearne** from Old English, meaning a 'dweller in a nook'; **Hern** could equally mean 'heron' (*see below*).

Heron, **Herron** from Middle English, meaning a 'heron' and probably applied to someone with long, thin legs like a heron's.

Herring from Old English, meaning a 'fish seller'.

Herst, **Hirst** from Old English, meaning a 'wood'.

Heston from Old English, meaning 'someone who lives by brushwood'.

Hetherington from Old English, meaning a 'heath dweller'.

Heward *see* **Howard**.

Hewer from Old English, meaning a 'stone/wood cutter'.

Heydon from Old English, meaning a 'hay hill'.

Hick, **Hicks** a diminutive form of 'Richard'.

Hickenbottom, **Higginbottom**, etc. from Old English, meaning a 'valley with oak trees'.

Hickock from Old English, probably a form of 'haycock'.

Hilbert *see* **Ilbert**.

Hildebrand from Old German, meaning 'battle sword'.

Hilder from Old English, meaning a 'dweller on a hill'.

Hill, **Hille**, **Hills** from Old English, meaning 'someone who lives on a hill'. Similarly, **Hillhouse** means 'someone who lives in the house on the hill', and **Hillman** 'someone who lives on a hill/ a hill man'.

Hillary from Latin, for someone 'cheerful'.

Hilton from Old English, meaning a 'farm on a hill/slope'.

Hindly, **Hindley** from Old English, meaning a 'wood populated with hinds'.

Hinton from Old English, meaning a 'farm in a high location'.

Hoad, **Hoath** from Old English, meaning a 'dweller on the heath'.

Hoar, **Hoare**, **Hore** from Old English, meaning 'grey-haired', or 'dweller by the bank'.

Hobart *see* **Hubert**.

Hobb, **Hobbes**, **Hobbs** diminutive forms of 'Robert'.

Hobday meaning 'a servant of Hobb'.

Hodd, **Hoddes**, **Hodds**, **Hodes**, **Hood**, **Hoods** from Old English, meaning a 'hood' and applied to a maker of hoods; **Hodder** is a 'hood-maker'.

Hodge, **Hodges** a pet form of 'Roger'.

Hogg from Old English, meaning a 'hog/pig', while **Hoggard**, **Hoggart**, **Hoggarth**, **Hoggett** is 'someone who tends to hogs'.

Holbech, **Holbeche** from Old English, meaning 'a stream in a ravine'.

Holbrook from Old English, meaning a 'brook in a ravine'. **Holden** is a 'dweller in a hollow valley'; **Holgate** is probably 'someone who lives by a road in a hollow'; **Holley**, **Holly** denotes a 'dweller by a clearing in a hollow'; **Holloway** meaning 'a road cut into a hollow' would have been the name of someone who lived near one, and **Holman** 'someone who lives in a hollow'.

Hollier, **Hollyer** from Middle English, meaning a 'debauchee'.

Hollister from Middle English, meaning a 'female keeper of brothels'.

Holm, **Holme** from Old Norse, meaning 'a dweller by the river flat/fen' (a 'holme' was a 'meadow surrounded by water').

Holt from Old English, meaning a 'wood'.

Holyoak from Old English, meaning a 'holy oak' or a 'gospel oak'.

Home, **Homes** from Old English, meaning 'someone who lives by a holm oak'.

Honey from Old English, meaning 'honey' and therefore referring to someone with a sweet nature.

Honeycomb, **Honeycombe** from Old English, meaning a 'dweller in a sweet/fertile valley'.

Hook, **Hooke**, **Hookes**, **Huck**, **Hucke**, **Hucks** from Old English, meaning 'crooked' and probably referring to someone with a crooked nose or bent back.

Hooker from Old English, and Middle English, meaning a 'maker of hooks'.

Hooper from Old English, meaning a 'maker of hoops' most likely for fitting round barrels and casks.

Hope from Old English, meaning a 'resident near an enclosed valley'.

Hopton from Old English, meaning a 'place in a valley/gorge'.

Hopwood from Old English, meaning a 'wood in a valley'.

Horden from Old English, meaning a 'dirty valley'.

Horder from Old English, meaning a 'hoarder' and probably denoting someone whose job it was to keep provisions, treasure, etc.

Horn, **Horne** from Old English, meaning 'someone living by a spur of land'.

Horrocks from Old Norse, possibly meaning a 'pile of stones'.

Horsley from Old English, meaning a 'pasture with horses'.

Horton from Old English, meaning a 'muddy/dirty place'.

Hosier either from Old English, meaning a 'maker of stockings', or Old French, meaning a 'maker of shoes'.

Hough from Old English, meaning a 'hill/rise'.

How, **Howe**, **Howes** from Old Norse, meaning 'someone who lives near a hill/burial site'.

Howard, **Heward** from Old French, meaning 'heart brave', but could also be a corruption of 'Hayward' (*see* p 65) or come from the Old English word for 'someone who tends a ewe herd or hog herd'.

Hoyle from Old English, meaning a 'hollow'.

Hubert, **Hubbard**, **Hubbart**, **Hobart** from Old German, meaning 'mind bright'.

Hull from Old English, meaning a 'hill'.

Hurley from Old English, meaning a 'wood or clearing'.

Husband from Old English, meaning a 'husbandman, farmer'.

Hussey, **Hussy**, **Husey** from Middle English, meaning a 'mistress of a house, a housewife'.

Huston from Old English, meaning a 'place with a house'.

Huxley from Old English, meaning a 'clearing'.

Hyde from Old English, a hide – a measurement of land more or less equal to a hundred acres.

Ick, Icke a diminutive form of 'Richard'.

Iden from Old English, meaning a 'woodland'.

Idle, Idel from Old English, meaning 'lazy' and perhaps referring to someone with unprofitable land.

Ilbert, Hilbert from Old German, meaning 'battle glorious'.

Iles, Isles from Old French, meaning a 'resident of the isle'.

Imberey, Imrie *see* **Amery**.

Impey, Impy from Old English, meaning an 'orchard enclosure'.

Ingham probably meaning 'Ing's homestead' (Ing being a Norse god descended from Odin).

Ingle from Old English, meaning a 'valley dweller'.

Inglebright from Old German, meaning 'angel bright/glorious'.

Ingleby from Old Norse, probably meaning a 'farm belonging to an Englishman'.

Ingram, Ingrams there are two quite different meanings to this name. The first is from Old English, meaning 'pastureland', while the second is from Old French, meaning an 'angel raven'.

Inman from Old English, meaning a 'keeper of an inn'.

Inwood, Innwood from Old English, meaning a 'dweller by the home-wood'.

Iremonger, Ironmonger from Old English, meaning an 'ironmonger'.

Ironside from Old English, meaning 'iron-side' and usually referring to a warrior or soldier.

Irwin, Irwine, Irwing *see* **Erwin**.

Isaac, Isaacs, Isacke, Isaacson from Hebrew, meaning 'laugh'. The name was not confined to the Jewish population, but was in wide use.

Issard, Izzard, Ezard from Old German, meaning 'ice battle'.

Isham from Old Welsh and Old English, meaning a 'place on the River Ise'.

Ivers meaning 'son of Ivor'.

Ivor, Ivers from Old Norse, meaning 'yew/bow army'.

Jack, Jacks, Jagg, Jaggs, Jakes all diminutives of 'John', from 'Jankin'; or of 'James', via 'Jacob' or 'Jacques'.

Jackman from Old English, meaning a 'servant of Jack'.

Jacob, Jacobs from Hebrew, meaning 'he supplanted'. This name was in use both before and after the Conquest.

Jaggar, Jaggars, Jagger, Jaggers from Old English, meaning a 'pedlar/hawker'. In medieval England the 'jagger' was someone who moved about the countryside, peddling goods.

Jago a form of 'Jacob' or 'James'.

James a form of 'Jacob'.

Janson meaning a 'son of John'.

Jardin, Jardine from Old French, meaning a 'dweller near a garden' or a 'gardener'.

Jarrard, Jarratt, Jarred, Jarrett a diminutive form of 'Gerald'.

Jarrod *see* **Gerald**.

Jay, Jaye from Old French, meaning a 'jay bird' and probably applied to people who chattered a lot.

Jeeves meaning 'son of Genevieve'.

Jeff, Jeffe, Jeffes, Jeffs diminutives of 'Geoffrey'.

Job, Jopp, Jupp from Hebrew, meaning 'one who is hated'.

Joel from the two names of God in Hebrew 'Yah' and 'El', or Old Breton, meaning 'the lord is generous'.

John from Hebrew, meaning 'one whom God/Yahweh has favoured'.

Jolley, Jollie, Jolly from Old French, meaning 'happy/cheerful'.

Jones meaning 'son of John'.

Jordan from Hebrew, meaning 'flowing downwards' and the name of the River Jordan, which was used as a Christian name by many Crusaders. **Judd** is probably a diminutive of 'Jordan'.

Joseph from Hebrew, meaning 'may God add'.

Joshua from Hebrew, meaning 'God is generous'.

Joy from Old French, meaning 'joy'.

Joyce possibly a mix of Old French words meaning 'joy' and 'jocund'.

Just from Latin, meaning 'just/righteous'.

Juster from Old French, meaning a 'jouster'.

Kay, Kaye, Kayes, Keay, Keays Keeys, Key, Keye, Keyes, Keys, Keyse there are several different meanings to this name. It may be from the Latin *Caius* meaning 'rejoicing'; it may come from Old French, meaning a 'quay' and applying to someone who worked by a wharf or dock; or it may come from Old Norse, meaning a 'jackdaw'.

Kear from Old English, meaning a 'maker of keys'.

Keat, Keate, Keates, Keats from Old English, meaning a 'hut/outhouse' most likely for cattle or sheep.

Kedge, Ketch from Old English, meaning someone who is 'lively'.

Keech from Middle English, meaning a 'butcher'.

Keen, Keene from Old English, meaning 'astute/sharp/brave'.

Keep from Middle English, meaning a 'stronghold/the innermost tower of a castle'.

Keeper as the above or meaning a 'jailer'.

Kelly, Kelley, Kellie from Irish 'O'Kelly', meaning a 'descendant of war', or from Cornish, meaning a 'wood/clearing'.

Kelman from Middle English, meaning a 'ship' and probably denoting a 'maker of keels'.

Kemble, Kimble from Old Welsh, meaning 'chief war'.

Kemp from Old English, meaning a 'warrior'.

Ken, Kenn from Old French, meaning a 'dog'.

Kennaway, Kenway, from Old English, meaning a 'bold war'.

Kennedy from O'Cinnéide, Irish Gaelic, meaning 'descendant of Cinnéide' ('ugly head'). Originating in County Clare, the Kennedys spread as far south as Wexford, which is from where the late US President J. F. Kennedy's family came.

Kennington from Old English, meaning a 'royal farm'.

Kennish a Manx contraction of 'MacAngus' – 'son of Angus'.

Kenrick from Old Welsh, meaning 'hero'.

Kenward from Old English, meaning a 'brave/bold guardian'.

Kermode a Manx version of 'MacDermot'.

Keswick from Old English, meaning a 'farm where cheese is made'.

Kettle from Old Norse, meaning a 'cauldron'.

Kew from Old French, meaning a 'cook' and probably applied to a keeper of an eating establishment.

Kiddell, Kiddle from Old French, meaning a 'fish-trap'.

Kidder from Middle English, meaning a 'maker/seller of faggots'.

Kidman from Middle English, meaning someone who looked after 'young goats, or kids'.

Killip a Manx contraction of 'MacPhilip' – 'son of Philip'.

Kilpatrick from Irish and Scots Gaelic, meaning the 'church of Patrick'.

Kilpin from Old English, meaning a 'calf enclosure'.

Kingsbury from Old English, meaning a 'king's manor house'; likewise, **Kingsford** is a 'king's ford', and **Kingsley** a 'king's wood/copse'.

Kinman from Old English, meaning a 'herdsman'.

Kinsey from Old English, meaning a 'royal victory'.

Kipps from Old English, meaning 'swollen' and probably applied to someone who was rotund/fat.

Kirk from Old Norse, meaning 'church', and denoting someone who lived next to one. It prefixes a number of place- and surnames, among them **Kirkham**, meaning a 'village church' or a 'village with a church'; **Kirkpatrick**, meaning a 'church of (Saint) Patrick', and **Kirkwood**, meaning a 'wood by a church' or a 'wood belonging to the church'.

Kitchen, **Kitchener**, **Kitchenor**, **Kitchiner**, **Kitchin**, **Kitching** from Old English, meaning a 'person who works in a kitchen' (and in particular the man who turned the spit).

Kitter from Middle English, meaning a 'maker of kits' (i.e. tubs and pails).

Knapp from Old English, meaning a 'hilltop', hence **Knapman** denoted someone who lived on or near one.

Knatchbull from Middle English, meaning 'to knock out bulls' i.e. the man who killed bulls for their meat – probably applied to butchers.

Knell from Old English, meaning 'someone who lived by the knoll'.

Knock from Scots and Irish Gaelic, meaning a 'small hill/hillock'.

Knoll from Old English, meaning a 'hilltop'.

Knott from Old Norse, meaning a 'knot' and probably used to describe a thickset person.

Knowling from Old English, meaning 'someone who lives at the top of a hill'.

Knox meaning 'from the family of Knock' (*see above*).

Lace from Middle English, meaning a 'cord' and used to denote a maker of cords/ribbons etc.

Lachlan from Scots Gaelic, for a 'lake'.

Ladd, **Ladds** from Middle English, meaning a 'man of low birth/a servant'.

Laing, **Laird** a Scots form of 'landlord/lord/master'.

Lakeman from Old English, meaning a 'dweller by a lake/watercourse'.

Laker either from Old English, meaning 'someone who lives by a stream', or from Old Norse, meaning an 'actor/one who plays games'.

Lamb, **Lambe**, **Lamm** from Old English, meaning a 'lamb' and probably applied either to someone who was 'meek in temperament' or to someone who 'tended lambs'.

Lambard, **Lambart**, **Lambarth**, **Lambert**, **Lampart**, **Lampert**, from Old German, meaning 'land bright', or from Old English, meaning 'lamb herd'.

Lambley from Old English, meaning a 'pasture for lambs'.

Lammond, **Lamond**, **Lamont** from Old Norse, meaning a 'lawman'.

Lampitt from Old English, meaning 'someone who lives by a clay pit'.

Land from Middle English, meaning a 'glade'.

Lander, Landers *see* **Lavender**.

Landray, Landrey, Landry from Old French, meaning a 'land ruler'.

Landseer from Old English, meaning a 'landmark'.

Lang, Lange from Old English, meaning 'long/tall', hence names like **Langdale** 'long valley'; **Langdon** 'long hill'; **Langford** 'long ford'; **Langham** 'long homestead', and **Langridge** 'long ridge' for people who lived in, on or near such places.

Lank from Old English, meaning 'tall/skinny/thin'.

Lappin, Lapping from Old French, meaning a 'rabbit' and probably denoting someone who bred rabbits for meat.

Lardner from Old French, denoting an 'officer in charge of pig food'.

Lark, Larke from Old English, meaning a 'lark' and probably denoting someone who was good at singing.

Larkin a diminutive of the name 'Laurence'.

Lascelles from Old French, meaning a 'hermitage'.

Last from Old English, meaning a 'last' (a wooden mould of a foot for the making of shoes).

Latch from Old English, meaning a 'wet place'.

Latchford from Old English, meaning a 'ford at a wet place/stream'.

Latham from Old English, meaning 'someone who lived by/next to the barns'.

Latimer, Lattimer, Lattimore from Old French, meaning an 'interpreter' (literally a speaker of Latin) or a 'letter-writer'.

Lauder from Scots Gaelic, meaning 'grey water'.

Laurie a diminutive form of 'Laurence'.

Lavender, Lander, Landers from Old French, meaning 'one who washes/a laundry woman'.

Law, Lawes, Laws either a diminutive of 'Laurence', or Old English for a 'burial mound'.

Lawless from Middle English, meaning 'unbridled/lawless'.

Lawton from Old English, meaning a 'place on a hillside'.

Lax from Old Norse, meaning a 'salmon'.

Layer from Old French, meaning 'the heir'.

Layland, Leyland from Old English, meaning 'unploughed land'.

Leach, Leech from Old English, for 'leech' and applied to those who used leeches, i.e. doctors.

Leadbeater, Leadbetter from Old English, meaning a 'worker in lead'.

Leak, Leake from Old English, meaning a 'stream'.

Leaf, Leafe from Old English, meaning 'dear one/beloved'.

Leaper from two different Old English words, one meaning a 'dancer', the other a 'basket weaver'.

Leat, Leate, Leates from Old English, meaning a 'dweller by the leat/stream'.

Leavey, Levey, Levi, Levy from Old English, meaning 'beloved soldier', or from the Hebrew word meaning 'one who is pledged/joined'.

Ledger, Leger from Old German, meaning a 'people spear'.

Leeford from Old English, meaning 'the ford at the shelter'.

Legat, Legate, Legatt, Leggat, Leggate, Leggatt, Leggett from Old French, meaning an 'ambassador'.

Legg, Legge from Old English, meaning 'someone who lives on a leg/neck of land' or from an archaic form of the word 'leigh' meaning a 'meadow'. Finally it might be from Old English, meaning a 'leg' and referring to a 'hosier'.

Leighfield from Old English, meaning 'pastureland'.

Leighton from Old English, meaning a 'bright hill'.

Lemmer from Old English, meaning 'people famous'.

Leo, Leon from Greek and Latin, meaning 'lion'.

Leonard, Lenard, Lennard from Old German, meaning 'lion bold'.

Lestrange *see* **Strange**.

Letcher from Old French, meaning a 'lecher'.

Lettice from Latin *laetitia* meaning 'joyful, glad'.

Leuty from Old French, meaning 'someone who is loyal'.

Lever, Levers, Leaver from Old English, meaning a 'reed' and no doubt referring to someone who worked with reeds.

Leveridge from Old English, meaning a 'beloved ruler'.

Levet, Levett, Levitt, Leavitt from Old English, meaning 'beloved battle'.

Levi *see* **Leavey**.

Lew, Lewes from Old English, meaning 'someone who lives by the hill/mound'.

Lewis, Louis from Old Frankish, meaning a 'loud/famous battle'.

Lichfield from Old English, meaning a 'grey wood'.

Liddall, Liddel, Liddell, Liddle from Old English, meaning a 'river valley'. A common surname in Scotland.

Lidgate, Liggatt from Old English, meaning a 'swing gate'.

Light from Old English, meaning 'light/swift/quick' or 'light place' i.e. someone who lives in a light glade/wood/field etc.

Lightbody from Old English, meaning a 'little person'.

Lightfoot from Old English, meaning 'someone who is swift of foot/quick'.

Liley, Lilley, Lillie, Lilly from Old English, meaning a 'dweller by a flax field' although Liley could also be a diminutive of 'Elizabeth'.

Limer from Old English, meaning 'someone who whitewashes'.

Linacre, Linaker, Lineker from Old English and Latin, meaning a 'flax field'.

Lind, Lynde, Lynds from Old English, meaning a 'dweller by the lime tree'.

Lindridge from Old English, meaning a 'dweller by a lime-tree ridge'.

Lineham, Lynam, Lynham from Irish O'Laigheanáin, meaning 'descendant of Laidhghnean', a name meaning 'snow-birth'.

Ling from Old Norse, meaning 'heather' or Old English, meaning a 'dweller by a ridge'.

Linter from Middle English, meaning a 'worker with flax'.

Linton from Old English, meaning a 'hill on which flax grows'.

Lisle, Lyle from Old French, meaning 'someone who lives on the island'.

Lister from Middle English, meaning a 'dyer'.

Lithgow from Scots Gaelic, meaning 'a wet hollow'.

Little, Littell, Lytle, Lyttle from Old English, meaning 'little'. Hence **Littleboy, Littlechild, Littlejohn, Littlewood**, whose meanings are obvious, and **Littlebury** 'little fort' and **Littleton** 'little place'.

Litwin from Old English, meaning 'bright friend'.

Livingston, Livingstone from Old English, meaning a 'place of a dear friend'.

Lloyd, Lloyds from Welsh, meaning 'grey'.

Loader from Old English, meaning a 'loader/carrier' perhaps even a 'ferryman'.

Loan from Old English, meaning a 'dweller by a lane'.

Lock, Locke, Locks from Old English, meaning 'an enclosure' or a 'lock of hair' or from Middle English, meaning a 'river lock'.

Lockhart from Old English, meaning a 'herdsman of sheep or cattle/livestock'.

Locksmith from Old English, meaning a 'maker of locks'.

Lockwood from Old English, meaning an 'enclosed wood'.

Lodder from Old English, meaning a 'beggar'.

Loft, **Lofts** from Middle English, meaning an 'attic room'.

Lofthouse, **Loftus** from Old Norse, meaning 'someone who lives in a house with an upper floor/attic', though it probably refers to one of the places of either name.

Lomas, **Lomax** from Old English, meaning a 'pool/stretch of still water', probably referring to someone from the place of that name in Lancashire.

Lombard, **Lumbert** either meaning 'someone from Lombardy' (in Italy) or, occasionally, from the Germanic 'long beard'. The early Italian immigrants were in fact moneylenders and therefore the surname can also mean 'a banker'.

Long from Old English meaning 'long, tall', it has spawned a number of surnames: **Longden**, **Longdon**, meaning 'dweller by the long hill'; **Longfellow** 'a tall man'; **Longfield** a 'long field' or from the town name Langford/Longford; **Longford** a 'long ford'; **Longman**, **Langman** a 'tall man', and **Longstaff** meaning a 'long staff' and probably applied to a bailiff or constable i.e. those people who used long staffs in their work.

Lord from Old English, meaning a 'lord/master'.

Lorimer, **Lorrimer** from Old French, meaning a 'maker of bits and spurs for horses'. These were quite often beautifully crafted.

Loud, **Lowde** from Old English, meaning 'noisy'.

Louth from Old English, meaning 'someone who lives by a noisy stream'.

Love there are two quite different meanings to this name, from Old English, meaning 'love'; and from Old French, meaning 'wolf'.

Loveday from Old English, meaning a 'dear/beloved day'; other such names include **Lovegood** a 'dear/beloved god'; **Loveguard** a 'beloved spear'; **Lovejoy** 'joy in love'; **Lovelace** 'loveless'; **Lovelock, Loveluck** a 'love curl of hair' – sometimes applied to an artificial lock of hair.

Lovett from Old French, meaning a 'wolf cub'.

Low, Lowe, Lowes there are various meanings to this name: from Old French, meaning a 'wolf'; from Old Norse, meaning 'short/low', and from Old English, meaning a 'burial mound'.

Lowrey, Lowrie, Lowry is a diminutive form of 'Laurence'.

Ludbrook from Old English, meaning a 'loud brook/stream'.

Ludford from Old English, meaning a 'ford over a loud stream/river'.

Ludlow from Old English, meaning a 'hill by a loud stream/river'.

Luff from Old English, meaning 'dear one'.

Lumley from Old English, meaning a 'wooded clearing by a stretch of water/lake/pool'.

Lund from Old Norse, meaning a 'wood/grove'.

Lurey, Lurie from Middle English, meaning a 'place where ewers of water were kept' and probably denoting one who looked after that room.

Luther from Old French, meaning a 'lute player'.

Lutton from Old Welsh and Old English, meaning a 'farm with a pool'.

Luttrell from Old French, meaning an 'otter'.

Lydford from Old English, meaning a 'ford over a bubbling stream'.

Lyon from Latin, meaning a 'lion'.

Lynch, Linch from Irish 'O'Loingsigh', meaning 'descendant of Loingsigh (*loinseach* meaning 'sailor'), or Old English, meaning someone who 'lived by a hill'.

Mabb a diminutive form of Mabel.

Mable, **Mabley** a diminutive form of Anabel.

Mac, **Mc**, **and**, **rarely now**, **M'** are the Gaelic prefixes meaning 'son of'. In a process of 'Englishing', the prefix was in a number of cases dropped, although in more recent times there has been a trend towards reinstating the prefixes among some. There are thousands of surnames with a 'Mac' prefix. In many cases they mean quite simply 'son of Andrew' or 'son of William' – these have not been included as their meaning is clear. The handful included here have been included because the form of the name is unusual, or the name is unusual outside Scotland and Ireland, or if there is anything else of particular interest about the name. Where a translation of a Gaelic name was readily available, it has been incorporated. Thus, for example, MacCall is 'son of a warlord', rather than 'son of Cathmhaoil'. All the names are under 'Mac' on the understanding that 'Mac' and 'Mc' are interchangeable.

MacAllaster, **Alaster**, **Allister** from Scots Gaelic, meaning 'son of Alexander'.

MacAlpin, **Alpine** from Scots Gaelic, meaning 'son of Alpin'.

MacBeath, **Beth** from Scots Gaelic, for 'son of Life'.

MacBride from Scots Gaelic, for 'son of a devotee of Saint Bridget'.

MacCall from Scots Gaelic, for 'son of a warlord'.

MacCallum from Scots Gaelic, meaning 'son of a worshiper of Saint Columba'.

MacCarthy from Irish, meaning 'son of Craddock' (*see* **Craddock**).

MacCaw from Irish and Scots Gaelic, meaning 'son of Adam'.

MacCloy from Scots Gaelic, meaning 'son of Lewis'.

MacComb, **Combe**, **Combie** from Scots Gaelic, meaning 'son of Thomas'.

MacConnal, **Connel** from Scots Gaelic, meaning 'son of Conall'.

MacCormack from Irish and Scots Gaelic, meaning 'son of Chariot Lad'.

MacCoy from Irish Gaelic, meaning 'son of Aodh' ('son of Hugh')

MacCrum from Scots Gaelic, meaning 'son of the bent one'.

MacCulloch from Scots Gaelic, meaning 'son of the Boar'.

MacDairmid, **Dearmid**, **Dermid**, **Dermit**, **Dermott** from Irish and Scots Gaelic, meaning 'son of Freeman'.

MacDonaugh from Scots Gaelic, meaning 'son of Duncan'.

MacEachan from Scots Gaelic, meaning 'son of a horse lord'.

MacElfrish from Scots Gaelic, meaning 'son of a worshipper of Saint Brice'.

MacEwan, **Ewen**, **Ewing** from Scots Gaelic, for 'son of Ewan'.

MacFarlan, **Farland** from Scots Gaelic, meaning 'son of Parlan'.

MacGee from Irish Gaelic, meaning 'son of Aodh'. (Sometimes written **Magee**.)

MacGenis from Scots Gaelic, for 'son of Angus'.3

MacGill from Scots Gaelic, meaning 'son of a stranger'.

MacGoldrick from Irish, meaning 'son of a High Templar'.

MacGowan from Irish and Scots Gaelic, meaning 'son of Smith'.

MacGuinness from Irish, meaning 'son of Angus'.

MacIlroy from Scots and Irish Gaelic, meaning 'son of a red-haired man'.

MacInnes from Scots Gaelic, meaning 'son of Angus'.

MacIntyre from Scots Gaelic, meaning 'son of a carpenter'.

MacKeith from Scots Gaelic, meaning 'son of Wolf'.

MacKenna from Irish, meaning 'son of Cionaodh'.

MacKenzie from Scots Gaelic, meaning 'son of Comely'.

MacKillop from Scots Gaelic, meaning 'son of Philip'.

MacKinlay, **Kinley** from Scots Gaelic, meaning 'son of Finlay'.

MacKinnon from Scots Gaelic, meaning 'son of the fair one'.

MacLachlan from Scots Gaelic, meaning 'son of Lachlan'.

MacLaren from Scots Gaelic, meaning 'son of Laurence'.

MacLean from Scots Gaelic, meaning 'son of a worshipper of Saint John'.

MacLeish from Scots Gaelic, meaning 'son of a devotee of Jesus'.

MacMahon from the Irish, meaning 'son of Bear'.

MacManus from the Irish, meaning 'son of Magnus'.

MacMaster from Scots Gaelic, meaning 'son of the master'.

MacMichael from Scots Gaelic, meaning 'son of a devotee of Saint Michael'.

MacNab from Scots Gaelic, meaning 'son of the abbot'.

MacNamara from the Irish, meaning 'son of the Sea Hound'.

MacOmish from Scots Gaelic, meaning 'son of Thomas'.

MacPherson from Scots Gaelic, meaning 'son of the parson'.

MacQueen from Scots Gaelic, meaning 'son of good/pleasant' (**Sweeney** is the Irish version.).

MacRobb from Scots Gaelic, for 'son of Robert'.

MacRory from Irish and Scots Gaelic, for 'son of the Red King'.

MacTaggart from Scots Gaelic, meaning 'son of the priest'.

MacTavish from Scots Gaelic, meaning 'son of Tammas' (Thomas).

MacVicar from Scots Gaelic, meaning 'son of the vicar'.

Macey, **Macy** *see* **Massey**.

Maddock, **Maddocks**, **Maddox** from Old Welsh, meaning 'goodly/beneficent'.

Madeley from Old English, meaning 'a clearing in a wood'.

Maddison, **Madison** meaning 'son of Matthew'.

Madge, **Maggs** meaning 'son of Margaret'. In Greek Margaret means 'pearl'.

Mager *see* **Mauger**.

Magnus from Latin, meaning 'great'; **Magnusson**, of course, is 'son of Magnus'.

Mahon from Irish, meaning a 'bear'.

Maidwell from Old English, meaning 'someone who lives by the maidens' well'.

Mailer, **Mailler** from Middle English, meaning an 'enameller'.

Mainwaring from Old French, meaning a 'dweller at Warin's manor' ('Warin' was a popular Norman first name).

Mair from Scots Gaelic, meaning an 'officer/king's herald'.

Makepeace from Old English, and Old French, meaning a 'maker of the peace/arbiter'.

Makin, **Makins**, **Meaken**, **Meakin**, **Meakins** meaning a 'little maid'.

Malcolm, **Malcom** from Scots Gaelic, meaning a 'devotee of St Columba'.

Malden, **Maldon** from Old English, meaning a 'cross/monument'.

Malleson meaning 'son of Malin'; 'Malin' was a diminutive of 'Mary'.

Mallory from Old French, meaning an 'unfortunate person'.

Malter from Old English, meaning either a 'maker of malt' or from Old French, meaning 'poor/unproductive ground'.

Malthouse from Old English, probably denoting the person who looked after the malthouse.

Malton from Old English, meaning the 'middle place/position'.

Man, **Mann**, **Manning** from Old English, and Old Norse, meaning a 'man'.

Manby from Old Norse, meaning a 'man's farm/homestead'.

Mander from Middle English, meaning 'beggar' or 'basket-maker'.

Manger, **Monger** from Old English, meaning a 'trader'.

Manners originally a Norman name, de Meyners, for someone who came from Mesnières in Normandy.

Mansfield from Old English, meaning a 'dweller next to the field by a hill'.

Mantel, **Mantell**, **Mantle** from Old French, meaning a 'cloak'.

Manwood from Old English, meaning 'someone who lives close to a common wood'.

Maples from Old English, meaning a 'dweller by the maples'.

Marber, **Marbler** from Old French, meaning 'someone who quarries/carves marble'.

March from Old English, meaning a 'dweller by a boundary' or someone from the Marches or borderlands (either between England and Wales or between England and Scotland).

Marden, **Mardon** from Old English, meaning a 'hill by the boundary'.

Mariner, **Marriner** from Old French, meaning a 'sailor'.

Marjoribanks from Old English, meaning 'someone who lives near a hillside'.

Marker there are several different meanings to this name. It could come from Old German, meaning a 'boundary marker'; it could originate in Old English, meaning 'a marker/embroiderer', or it could refer to another Old English word meaning a 'writer'.

Marland from Old English, meaning a 'lake', or from Old French, meaning someone who quarried 'marl' (a kind of rock).

Marlow, **Marlowe** from Old English, meaning 'that which is left over after a pond or pool has been drained'.

Marr, **Marrs** from Old Norse, meaning a 'pool/marsh'.

Marriott a diminutive form of 'Mary'.

Marrow, **Marrows** from Middle English, meaning a 'loved one/ companion/lover'.

Marsh from Old English, meaning a 'dweller near a marsh'.

Marshall, **Maskell**, **Maskill** from Old French, meaning a 'person who tends to horses/groom/farrier'.

Marsham from Old English, meaning 'someone who lives by a marsh'. Similarly, **Marshfield**, meaning a 'field by a marsh', and **Marston**, meaning a 'house by a marsh'.

Marter, **Martyr** from Middle English, meaning a 'weasel'.

Marval, **Marvell** from Old French, meaning 'wonderful'.

Marwood from Old French, meaning 'someone who dwells by the big wood'.

Mason from Old French, meaning a 'stonemason'.

Massey, **Massie**, **Macey**, **Macy** a diminutive of 'Matthew', but can also be from Old French, meaning a 'hill range'.

Massinger *see* **Messenger**.

Mather, **Mathers** a pet form of the name 'Matthew'.

Matlock from Old English, meaning 'an oak tree round which meetings are held'.

Matter, **Matters** from Old French, meaning a 'mattress maker'.

Mauger, **Mager**, **Major** from Old German, meaning a 'council spear'.

Maurice, **Morris** from Latin meaning 'moorish/swarthy' and applied to those of a dark complexion.

Maw, **Mawe**, **Mawes** this surname has several different meanings. First, it can originate from Old Norse, meaning a 'sea mew'; it may be from Old English, meaning a 'meadow'. Finally it may come from Middle English, meaning a 'female relative/relative by marriage'.

Mawer, **Mower** from Old English, meaning 'someone who mows'.

Maxton from Scots Gaelic meaning a 'farm'.

Maxwell from Scots Gaelic, meaning a 'well'.

May, **Maye**, **Mayes**, **Mays**, **Mey**, **Meye**, **Meys** from Old English, meaning a 'young girl or boy'.

Mayer, **Mayers**, **Mayor**, **Meyer**, **Meyers** there are several different meanings to this name. Firstly it may come from Old French, meaning 'mayor' or it might come from Middle English, meaning a 'physician'. It may also come from Old English, meaning 'someone who lived by a mere or pool'.

Mayfield from Old English, meaning a 'field overgrown with maygrass'.

Mayhew from 'Matthew'.

Meader from Old English, meaning 'mead' and referring to 'a maker/seller of mead'.

Meadow, **Meadows** from Old English, meaning 'someone who lives by the meadow'.

Meadway, **Medway** from Old English, meaning a 'dweller by the river Medway'.

Mear, **Meare** from Old English, meaning a 'pool/boundary of a pool'.

Medcraft from Old English, meaning a 'dweller by the croft at the meadow'.

Medwin from Old English, meaning a 'reward of mead'.

Meek, **Meeke**, **Meeks** from Middle English, meaning 'humble'.

Meese from Old English, meaning 'moss'.

Meikle from Scots dialect, meaning 'big'.

Mellon from the French town of Meulan, a name which probably came with the Norman invasion.

Meller from Old French, meaning 'someone who collects the honey'.

Mellor, **Mellors** probably from Middle English, meaning a 'barren hill'.

Melton from Old English, meaning a 'middle farm'.

Melville this surname usually derives from the town 'Melville' which itself was named by Geoffrey de Mallaville who came from Emalleville.

Mendoza from Spanish, meaning a 'mountain'.

Menzies a Scots version of the name 'Manners' (in Scots the name is pronounced 'Mingies').

Mercer, **Mercier** from Old French, meaning a 'merchant' and usually applied to a trader of fabric.

Meredith from Old Welsh, meaning a 'lord'.

Merry means . . . merry; **Merriman** is a 'merry man', while **Merryweather** means 'fair weather'.

Merton from Old English, meaning a 'dweller by a lake'.

Messenger, Massinger from Old French, meaning a 'messenger/courier'.

Metcalf, Metcalfe, Medcalf, Medcalfe from Old English, meaning a 'calf that is to be fattened for slaughter/eating'.

Mew from Old English, meaning a 'seagull' or from Old French, meaning a 'cage for keeping hawks'.

Meynell from Old French, meaning 'habitation' (usually of a nobleman).

Michie a Scottish diminutive of 'Michael'.

Micklethwaite from Old Norse, meaning a 'big meadow or enclosed piece of land'.

Middle from Old English, meaning 'middle' and probably denoting someone who lived in the centre of the village/town. More common are the specific 'Middles': **Middlebrook** meaning a 'dweller by the central brook'; **Middlemass, Middlemiss** meaning the 'middlemost'; **Middleton** meaning the 'middle farm' and **Middlewood** meaning the 'middle wood'.

Midwinter from Old English, meaning 'someone who was born/baptized at Christmas' i.e. in midwinter.

Mighty from Old English, meaning 'mighty/strong'.

Milbourn, Milburne from Old English, meaning 'dweller by the mill stream'.

Mildmay from Old English, meaning 'one who is a gentle maiden'.

Miles, Myles from the Latin meaning a 'soldier'; **Millsom, Millson** are 'son of Miles'.

Millar, Scots version of **Miller**, meaning 'miller'. There are a number of mill-related names from Old English, including **Millhouse, Milhouse** meaning someone who lives at a 'mill house'; **Millham** meaning a 'house with a mill'; **Millington** for one who lives at a farm with a mill; **Millman** for one employed at a mill; **Millward, Millard, Millwood** meaning a keeper of a mill, a miller; **Milner** meaning a 'miller'; **Mills** meaning 'someone who lives by the mills', and **Milton** meaning a 'mill farm'.

Miner, **Miners**, **Minor**, **Minors** from Old French, meaning a 'miner'.

Minet, **Minett** from Old French, meaning 'someone who is delightful'.

Mingay, **Mingey** a Breton name meaning a 'stone dog'.

Minogue, **Minnock**, **Manogue** from Irish O'Muineog, meaning 'descendant of Muineog' (which might in some cases derive from *manach* 'monk').

Minter from Old English, meaning a 'maker of money'.

Minster from Old English, meaning a 'church/monastery'.

Mitcham from Old English, meaning a 'large homestead/farmstead'.

Mitchel, **Mitchell**, **Michell** either a diminutive form of 'Michael' (**Mitchelson**, etc., means 'son of Michel/Michael'), or from Old English, meaning 'big/large' etc. – as in **Mitchelmore**, meaning one who dwells on or by a 'big moor'.

Mitford from Old English, meaning 'middle of the ford'.

Mitton from Old English, meaning 'someone who lives in the middle of the village'.

Moat, **Mote** from Middle English, meaning 'someone who lives in or near a castle'.

Moffat, **Moffett** from Scots Gaelic, meaning a 'long piece of land'.

Mogg most likely a diminutive form of 'Margaret'.

Moir from Scots Gaelic, meaning 'big'.

Molin, **Molins** from Old French, meaning a 'resident by a mill'.

Molland from Old Welsh, meaning a 'piece of farmland near a barren hill'.

Molloy from **O'Molloy**, Irish Gaelic, meaning a 'descendant of the great and noble leader'.

Moloney, **Molony** from **O'Moloney**, Irish Gaelic, meaning a 'descendant of the church'.

Molton from Welsh, meaning a 'farm by a bare hill'.

Monday, **Mondy** from Old English, meaning a 'person born on a Monday'.

Moneypenny from Old English, meaning someone with 'many a penny'.

Monger *see* **Manger**.

Monk, **Monck** from Old English, meaning a 'monk' and used either to denote a person from a monastery or in jest.

Monkton from Old English, meaning a 'farm belonging to monks'.

Montgomerie, **Montgomery** most likely from a powerful Norman family, de Montgomery, from near Lisieux in Calvados, where there are neighbouring villages called Sainte-Foy-de-Montgommery and Saint-Germain-de Montgommery. Normans of that name settled across the British Isles, especially in Ireland, Scotland and Wales, where they gave their name to Montgomeryshire (now part of Powys).

Moodey, **Moody** from Old English, meaning someone who was 'bold/brave'.

Moon, **Moone**, **Munn** from Old French, meaning a 'monk'.

Moorby from Old Norse, meaning a 'farm on the fens'.

Moor, **Moore**, **Moores**, **Moors**, **More**, **Mores** from Latin and Old French, meaning a 'Moor' i.e. someone of swarthy complexion.

Moorcroft from Old English, meaning a 'croft by a moor'. **Moorhouse**, **Morehouse**, **Morres** mean a 'house on the moor', while **Moorwood** means a 'wood on the moor', **Mooring** 'someone who lives on the moor', and **Moorshead** 'someone who lives on the edge of the moor'.

Morel, **Morell**, **Morrell** from Old French, meaning of 'brown/swarthy' complexion.

Morgan a very old Celtic name, meaning 'sea-bright'.

Morland from Old English, meaning a 'dweller on a moor'; similarly, **Morley** would denote one who lived in a 'clearing on a moor', and **Morton** a 'dweller at a moor farm'.

Mortimer from Old French, meaning a 'dead sea/lake'.

Mortlock from Old English, meaning a 'stream with young salmon'.

Mosely from Old English, meaning a 'clearing in a wood'.

Moss either a diminutive of 'Moses', or from Old English, meaning a 'swamp'.

Mothersole, **Mothersill** from Old English, meaning 'a proud soul'.

Mount, **Mounter** from Old English, meaning 'someone who lives near the hill'.

Moyle from Cornish meaning a 'bald person'.

Moyne from Old French, meaning a 'monk'.

Much, **Muckle** from Old English, meaning 'big'.

Mudd most likely a derivative of the name 'Maud'.

Muir from Old English, meaning a 'dweller on the moor', hence **Muirhead** meaning 'someone who lives at the top of the moor', both names common in Scotland.

Mumford from Old French, meaning a 'strong hill'.

Munday, **Mundie**, **Mundy** from Old Norse, meaning a 'protector'.

Munro, **Munroe**, **Munrow** from Old Irish, possibly meaning 'dweller by the mouth of the river Roe'.

Murch from Middle English, meaning a 'dwarf'.

Murchie, **Murchison** from Scots Gaelic, 'son of Murchadh' – i.e. 'son of Murdoch' (*see below*).

Murdoch, **Murdock** either of two names from Scots Gaelic: Muireach, meaning a 'seaman/mariner', and Murchadh, meaning 'sea warrior'.

Murgatroyd from Old English, meaning 'Margaret's clearing'.

Murphy from O'Murphy and MacMurphy, Old Irish, meaning 'descendant of a sea warrior'. A name made famous by the expression 'Murphy's Law', which states that if something can go wrong, it will.

Murray, **Murrey**, **Murrie**, **Murry** from the Scottish province of Moray (from the name 'de Moravia'), or from Middle English, meaning 'merry'.

Mutton from Old French, meaning 'sheep' and applied to a shepherd.

Myer, **Myers** from Old Norse, meaning a 'dweller by the marsh'.

Myerscough from Old Norse, meaning a 'dweller by a marshy wood'.

Nabb, **Nabbs** a diminutive of 'Robert'.

Naismith from Old English, meaning a 'knifesmith'.

Nance a Cornish name meaning a 'valley'.

Napier, **Naper**, **Napper** from Old French, meaning a 'table cloth' and probably referring to a maker of table linen.

Nares from Old French, meaning 'black'.

Nash from Old English, meaning a 'dweller by an ash tree'.

Nathan from Hebrew, meaning a 'gift'.

Nayler, **Naylor** from Old English, meaning a 'maker of nails'.

Naysmith from Old English, meaning a 'knife/nail smith'.

Neal, **Neale**, **Neele**, **Neil**, **Neill**, **Niel**, **Niell**, **Niles**, **Nigel** from Irish, meaning a 'champion', although also connected to the Latin *niger* meaning 'black'.

Neam, **Neame** from Old French, meaning a 'dwarf'.

Neat, **Neate** from Old English, meaning a 'herder of ox and cattle'.

Neave from Old English, meaning 'nephew'.

Needham from Old English, meaning a 'place struck by poverty'.

Needle, **Needler**, **Nelder** from Old English, meaning a 'maker of needles'.

Nelson from Old English, meaning 'son of Nell'.

Nesbit, Nesbitt, Naisbit a toponymic; the place name, from Old English, means a 'nose bite', a reference to a sharp bend in a river.

Ness from Old English, meaning 'someone who lives on a headland'.

Nessling from Old English, meaning a 'nestling/youngster'.

Netherton from Old English, meaning a 'lower farm dweller'; and, similarly, **Netherwood** is a 'lower wood dweller'.

Nettleton from Old English, meaning a 'place overgrown with nettles'.

Neven, Nevins, Niven from the Irish, meaning a 'little saint'.

Neville from Old French, meaning a 'new place'.

New from Old English, meaning 'new/newcomer'. Among other 'New' names are **Newbiggin** meaning a 'new building'; **Newbrough** a 'new town/market town'; **Newcomb, Newcombe** meaning 'someone who has newly arrived/newcomer'; **Newey, Neway** a 'dweller by the new enclosure'; **Newhall** 'someone who lives in the new hall/house'; **Newham** 'someone who lives at the new homestead'; **Newland** 'new land/newly acquired land'; **Newman, Nieman, Nyman** a 'new man/ newcomer'; **Newstead** a 'new farmstead', and **Newton** meaning a 'new place/village'.

Nightingale from Old English, meaning 'nightingale' and probably denoting someone with a beautiful singing voice.

Nixon meaning 'son of Nicholas'.

Noake, Noakes *see* **Oak**.

Nobbs a diminutive form of 'Robert'.

Noble, Nobles from Old French, meaning 'noble, famous'.

Nolan from O' Nolan, Irish Gaelic, meaning 'descendant of Nualláin' (*nuall* means 'shout').

Norman, Normand from Old French, meaning a 'Norman'.

Norris from Old French, meaning a 'Northener'.

North from Old English, meaning a 'dweller from the North/to the North'. 'North' names include **Norburn** meaning a 'dweller by the north stream'; **Norgate** meaning a 'north gate' (probably of a castle/town); **Northam** 'someone who lived by the north meadow'. **Northcliff**, **Northcliffe** a 'dweller by the north cliff'; **Northmore** a 'dweller by the north moor/fen'; **Northway**, **Norway** meaning 'someone who lived to the north of the road/way'; **Northwood**, **Norwood** meaning a 'dweller from the northern wood', and **Norwich** meaning a 'northern town'.

Nott from Old English, meaning 'bald/short-haired'.

Noy, **Noyce**, **Noyes** from Hebrew *Noah* meaning 'long-lived'.

Nunn, **Nunns** from Old English, meaning a 'nun' and used to describe someone with a demure nature; with the final *s* it could also have been applied to a servant at a nunnery.

Nunney, **Nunny** from Old English, meaning a 'dweller by a nunnery'.

Nutbeam, **Nutbeem** from Old English, meaning 'someone who lives near a nut tree'.

Nye from Old English, meaning a 'dweller by a stream'.

Oade, **Oades**, **Oddie**, **Oaten**, **Oates** from Old German, meaning 'riches'.

Oak, **Oake**, **Oaks**, **Oke**, **Noake**, **Noakes** from Old English, meaning an 'oak tree' and usually referring to someone who lived near an oak tree. Hence **Oakden** meaning a 'dweller in an oak valley', and **Oakley** meaning a 'dweller in an oak wood'.

O'Brien, **O'Bryan** from Irish, meaning a 'descendant of Brian' (that is, of King Brian Boru).

O'Connell from Irish, meaning a 'descendant of Connall' (meaning 'high powerful').

O'Conner from Irish, meaning a 'descendant of Conchobhar' (meaning 'high will').

Odger from Old German and Old French, meaning a 'spear carrier'.

O'Donnel from Irish, meaning a 'descendant of Donald'.

O'Donovan from Irish, meaning a 'descendant of Donndubhan' (meaning 'dark brown').

Ogilvie possibly from a Welsh/Gaelic mixture, meaning a 'high place'; an old Scottish name.

O'Grady from Irish, meaning a 'descendant of Grada' (meaning 'noble').

Old, **Olds**, **Ould**, **Oulds** from Old French, meaning 'senior/old'.

Olden *see* **Alden**.

Older *see* **Alder**.

Oldfield from Old English, meaning 'someone who dwelt by the old field'. Among other 'Olds' are **Oldman**, **Olman** meaning an 'old man'; **Oldreave**, **Oldrieve** meaning a 'senior official', and **Oldroyd** meaning 'someone who lived by the old wood clearing'.

Oldridge *see* **Aldridge**.

Oliver, **Olivier** most likely from Old French, meaning 'an olive branch'.

Ollerenshaw from Old English, meaning 'someone who lived close to a wood with alder trees'.

Oman, **Omond** from Old Norse, meaning a 'high protector'.

O'Mara, **O'Meara** from Irish, meaning a 'descendant of Meadhar' ('merry'). One of the few Irish names where the 'O'' prefix was not widely dropped.

O'Neal, **O'Neill** from Irish, meaning a 'descendant of Neal'.

Onion, **Onions** from Old French, meaning 'onion' and therefore applied to an onion-seller.

Orchard from Old English, usually applied to someone who worked in an orchard.

Ord, **Orde** from Old English, meaning a 'spear'.

Ordway from Old English, meaning a 'spear warrior'.

Ore, **Orr** from Old English, meaning a 'dweller on a bank or hillside'.

O'Reilly from Irish, meaning a 'descendant of Reilly' (meaning 'valiant').

Oriel from Old German, meaning 'fire-strife'.

Orledge from Old French for 'clock', and therefore applied to a maker of clocks.

Orme, **Ormes** from Old Norse, meaning a 'dragon/serpent'.

Ormiston from Old Norse, and Old English, meaning a 'dragon's farm'.

Orton from Old English, meaning 'someone who lives on/near a hill farm'.

Osborn, **Osborne**, **Osbourn**, **Osbourne** from Old Norse, meaning a 'god bear' and presumably applied to a great warrior.

Oscroft from Old English, meaning 'someone who lived by an ox farm'.

Osgood from Old English, meaning 'god of gods'.

Oslar, **Osler** from Old French, meaning 'someone who dealt in poultry'.

Osmond, **Osmund** from Old English, meaning a 'god protector'.

Ostler, **Hostler** Middle English, meaning an 'innkeeper'.

Ostridge from Old French, meaning a 'hawk' and probably referring to someone who worked with hawks.

Oswin from Old English, and Old Norse, meaning a 'god friend'.

Otter this name has two possible sources. It can either be from Old Norse, meaning a 'dread army', or from Middle English, meaning 'otter' and applied to a hunter of these creatures.

Outridge, **Outteridge**, **Uttridge** from Old English, meaning 'dawn-powerful'.

Ovens from Old English, meaning 'someone who worked the ovens/fires'.

Over from Old English, meaning a 'hillside'.

Owen, **Owens** *see* **Ewan**.

Owles from Old English, meaning 'an owl' and perhaps referring to a wise person.

Oxer, **Oxman** from Old English, both meaning someone who tended oxen.

Oxley from Old English, meaning a 'field for oxen'.

Oyler from Old French, meaning 'oil' and referring to a maker or dealer in oil.

Pace, **Pays**, **Peace** from Middle English, meaning 'peace/harmony'.

Pack, **Pakes** from Old French, meaning Easter, perhaps referring to someone born at that time. **Packard** has the same meaning ('(h)ard' is a common suffix in nouns and names).

Packer from Middle English, meaning, a 'packer' (probably of wool).

Pakeman, **Packman** from Middle English, meaning a 'pack/bundle' and probably referring to a 'pedlar' i.e. someone who carried a pack with him at all times.

Paddock from Old English, meaning a 'frog'.

Page, **Paige** from Old French, meaning a 'page-boy'.

Paget, **Pagett** from Old French, meaning a 'little page'.

Pain, **Paine**, **Paines**, **Pane**, **Panes**, **Payne**, **Paynes** from Latin meaning 'someone who lived in the countryside/a resident in a country village/a rustic'.

Painter from Old French, meaning a 'painter/artist'.

Paisley from Scots Gaelic, meaning a 'church' or 'graveyard'.

Paler from Old French, meaning a 'pan' and referring to a maker of pans/pots etc.

Palfrey, **Palfery** from Old French, meaning a 'saddle-horse'. Hence **Palfreyman**, **Palfreeman** meaning a 'man in charge of the saddle-horses'.

Pallis from Old French, meaning a 'fence/palisade' and referring, like the names **Palliser**, **Pallister**, to a maker of fences, etc., or to someone who lived near a fence.

Palmar, **Palmer** from Old French, meaning a 'pilgrim to the Holy Land' (who would return with a palm leaf as evidence of the fact that he had successfully made the journey).

Pankhurst a corruption of 'Pentecost', originally given as a Christian name to one born during that festival.

Pannell from Middle English, meaning a 'wainscot or saddle panel' and referring to a maker of panels.

Pannier from Old French, meaning a 'maker of baskets'.

Pardew, **Pardey** an Old French exclamation meaning 'By God!'

Parfett, **Parfit**, **Parfitt** from Old French, meaning a 'highly trained person'.

Pargeter, **Pargetter**, **Pargitter** from Old French, meaning a 'plasterer'.

Parham, **Perham**, **Perram** from Old English, meaning 'someone who lives near where pears are grown'.

Paris, **Parris**, **Parrish** this name has two possible derivations: it can mean, quite simply, a 'person from Paris', or it can derive from 'Paris', which was once a fairly common first name, and was the popular French form of the name 'Patrick'.

Park, **Parke**, **Parkes**, **Parks** from Old French, meaning a 'wooded enclosure'.

Parker, **Parkman** from Old French, meaning 'the man in charge of the park'.

Parkhouse from Old English, meaning 'dweller at the house in the park'.

Parkinson meaning 'son of **Perkin**'.

Parlour from Old French, meaning 'one who speaks', possibly denoting someone in the legal profession, although it may also mean a 'chatterbox'. It may also mean 'the parlour servant' – the servant who looked after the room in a monastery officially used for discussions, interviews and meetings – or perhaps someone who dealt in pearls, or made glass ones, e.g. for rosaries.

Parmenter, **Parminter**, **Parmeter** from Old French, meaning a 'tailor'.

Parnall, **Parnell** once used as a girl's Christian name, probably deriving from Petronilla, a feminine diminutive of the Latin name Petronius, or Peter.

Parr a diminutive form of 'Piers/Peter', as is **Parrell**.

Parry from Welsh 'ap Harry' meaning 'son of Harry'.

Parsloe, **Parslow**, **Parsley**, **Pasley** from Old French, meaning 'someone who lives across the water'.

Parson, **Parsons** from Old French, meaning a 'parson/priest'.

Partridge from Old French, and used to denote a 'keeper of partridges'.

Pascall, **Pascoe** from Latin, meaning anything 'connected with Easter'.

Pash, **Pashe**, **Paish**, **Pask**, **Paske** from Old French, meaning 'Easter' and probably referring to one born at that time.

Passant from Old French, meaning 'the one who goes ahead' and possibly denoting a herald.

Passmore, **Pasmore** from Old French, meaning 'cross the sea', and used to denote a sailor, traveller.

Patch from Middle English, meaning 'Easter'.

Paton a diminutive form of 'Patrick'.

Patterson, **Paterson**, **Pattison** meaning 'son of Patrick'.

Paul, **Paule**, **Pawle**, **Pole**, **Poles**, **Poll**, **Pool**, **Poole** from Latin *paulus* meaning 'small', although **Pool**, **Poole** may also mean 'someone who lives by a pool'.

Paulin, **Pawling** a diminutive of 'Paul'.

Pauncefoot, **Pauncefort** from Old French, meaning someone with a 'rounded stomach'.

Paxman, from Middle English, 'servant of Pack'.

Paw, **Pawe**, **Pea**, **Poe** from Old English, meaning a 'pea'.

Peacock from Old English, meaning a 'peacock' and probably describing a man of haughty disposition.

Peak, **Peake**, **Peek** from Old English, meaning a 'dweller on the peak'.

Pearce *see* **Piers**.

Pearl from Old French, meaning a 'pearl' and denoting a trader in pearls.

Pearman from Old English, meaning a 'grower/seller of pears'.

Pearson meaning 'son of Piers'.

Peascod, **Pescod**, **Peasgood** from Old English, meaning a 'pea-pod' and possibly denoting a seller of peas.

Peddar, **Pedder**, **Pedlar**, **Pedler** from Old French, meaning a 'pedlar'.

Peel, **Peele** from Old French, meaning a 'stake' and denoting someone who was tall, but also the name of certain towers (peel towers) built along the Scots/English border and therefore denoting someone sturdy.

Pegg a diminutive of 'Margaret'.

Pell, **Pells** a diminutive of 'Peter' but may also come from Old French, meaning 'skin' and thereby denoting a dealer of skins.

Peller from Old English, meaning an 'expensive cloak'.

Pellew, **Pellow** from Old French, meaning a 'wolf skin'.

Pelly from Old French, meaning a 'bald person'.

Pelter from Old French, meaning a 'skinner'.

Pendle from Old Welsh and Old English, meaning a 'hill'.

Pendor *see* **Pindar**.

Pengelly, Pengelley a Cornish surname meaning 'top of the wood/the main wood'.

Penn from Old English, meaning an 'enclosure/field'.

Pennant from Welsh, meaning a 'high valley' and denoting someone who lived in one.

Penner from Middle English, meaning 'someone who lives on a hill'.

Pennyfather, Pennefeather, Pennyfeather from Old English, meaning a 'miser' i.e. someone who 'fathered' his pennies.

Pennyman from Old English, meaning a 'servant of Penny'.

Penry, Pendry from Welsh 'ap Henry' meaning 'son of Henry'.

Pentland from Old Norse, meaning a 'dweller in the land of the Picts'.

Peploe, Peplow from Old English, meaning a 'stony hill'.

Pepper from Old English, meaning 'pepper' and denoting a dealer in pepper/spices.

Perceval, Percival from Old French, meaning 'pierce the valley'.

Peregrine from Latin meaning a 'pilgrim'.

Perkin, Parkin a diminutive of 'Peter', from which comes 'Parkinson'.

Perrier from Old French, meaning either a 'quarrier', or someone who lived near or tended pear trees.

Perriton from Old English, meaning a 'farm where pear trees are grown'.

Perry, Pirie from Old English, meaning a 'pear tree' and denoting someone who lived close to one.

Petch, **Petchey**, **Pechey** from Old French, meaning a 'sinful person'.

Peter, **Peters** from Greek and Latin meaning a 'rock', popular both as a Christian name and a surname. Its many diminutives are to be found especially among surnames.

Petrie, **Petry** a diminutive form of 'Peter'.

Pettegree, **Petticrew**, **Pettigrew** from Old French, meaning 'of little growth' and denoting a small person/dwarf/midget.

Pettifer, **Pettyfer**, **Petifer** from Latin and Old French, meaning someone with 'feet of iron' and possibly referring to an old soldier who had lost a foot in battle.

Pettit, **Pettitt**, **Petty** from Old French, meaning 'little/small'.

Peverall, **Peverell**, **Peverill** from Old French, meaning 'pepper' and referring to a dealer in spice.

Philcox a diminutive of 'Philip' plus 'Cox'.

Philip, **Philips** from Greek meaning a 'horse-lover'.

Philpot, **Philpots**, **Phipp**, **Phipps** diminutive forms of 'Philip'.

Physick from Old French, meaning 'medicine' and denoting a doctor.

Picker, **Pickers** from Old English, there are three possible meanings to this name. It may denote a 'maker or seller of wooden pikes', or it may mean a 'fishmonger/dealer in pike-fish', or it may refer to someone who dwelt on or by a hill.

Pickbourne, **Pickburn** from Old English, meaning a 'pike stream'. Similarly, **Pickford** probably denoted someone who lived near a ford over a river where there were pike – or it could mean a ford with wooden pikes.

Pickerell, **Pickerill** from Middle English, meaning a 'young pike'.

Pickett, **Picot**, **Piggot**, **Piggott** from Old French, meaning a 'pointed object.

Pickles from Middle English, meaning an 'enclosed piece of land/ field'.

Piddell from Old English, meaning a 'marshy field'.

Pidgen, **Pidgon**, **Pigeon** from Old French, meaning a 'pigeon' and denoting someone who is easily fooled out of their money i.e. easily plucked.

Piers, **Pierse**, **Pearce**, **Pears**, **Pearse**, **Peers**, **Peirce**, **Peirs**, **Peirse**, **Peres** from Old French, for 'Peter' (ultimately from Greek and Latin Petros/Petrus, meaning 'rock').

Pigg from Old English, meaning a 'pig' and denoting a keeper of these animals.

Pike, **Pyke** either from Old English, meaning a 'hilltop' or a 'pick-axe' or from Old French, meaning a 'pike' or sometimes a 'woodpecker'.

Pilch from Middle English, meaning a 'garment made from skin/fur'.

Pilcher (*see above*) a maker of pilches.

Pile, **Pyle** from Old English, meaning a 'maker of posts/stakes'.

Pill from Old English, meaning a 'little stream/brook'.

Pillar, **Piller**, **Pillers** from Old English, meaning 'someone who lives by the stream'; or 'someone who lives near a pillar or stake'; or – a less popular derivation – a 'plunderer, pillager'.

Pilling, **Pillings** from Old English, meaning 'someone who lives by a stream'.

Pinch *see* **Pink**.

Pinchbeck from Old English, meaning a 'stream with finches'.

Pincher from Middle English, meaning a 'haggler'.

Pindar, **Pinder**, **Pindor**, **Pendor** from Old English, meaning 'someone who impounds, shuts up' and thereby denoting a jailer or one whose job it was to round up and pen stray animals.

Pine from Old French, meaning a 'pine tree' – a nickname for a tall man.

Pinfold, **Penfold** from Old English, meaning 'one in charge of the pinfold', that is the 'pen or pound for fowl'.

Pink, **Pinck**, **Pinks**, **Pinch** from Old English, meaning a 'chaffinch'.

Pin, **Pinn**, **Pinner** from Old English, meaning a 'maker of pins/pegs'.

Pipe, **Pipes** from Old English, meaning a 'water pipe, stream or any type of conduit for water'.

Piper from Old English, meaning a 'pipe player'.

Pitcher, **Pitchers** from Old English, meaning 'someone who works with pitch/tar'.

Pitchford from Old English, meaning a 'ford near a place with pitch'.

Pitman, **Pittman** from Old English, meaning 'someone who lives in a pit/hollow'.

Pitt, **Pitts** from Old English, meaning a 'pit/hollow'.

Pizey, **Pizzey** *see* **Pusey**.

Place, **Plaice** from Old French, meaning a 'market or town square'.

Plater, **Platter** from Old English, meaning either a 'maker of armour plating', or, from 'plea' and 'plead', an 'advocate'.

Player from Old English, meaning an 'athlete'.

Pleasance, **Pleasaunce**, **Pleasants** from Old French, meaning 'pleasure' or 'pleasant'.

Plimpton from Old English, meaning a 'farm with plum trees'.

Plowman from Old English, meaning a 'ploughman'.

Plowwright from Old English, meaning a 'maker/seller of ploughs'.

Plum, **Plumb** from Old French, meaning 'lead' and denoting someone who worked with lead.

Plumley from Old English, meaning a 'place where plums grow'.

Poindexter from Old French, meaning the 'right fist'.

Pollard either comes from the name 'Paul', or from Middle English, meaning 'someone with a crop-head' – someone who habitually wears his hair cut very short.

Polson, **Poulson** meaning a 'son of Paul'.

Pomeroy, **Pomery** from Old French, meaning an 'apple orchard'.

Pomfret, **Pomfrett** from Latin *ponte fracto* meaning a 'broken bridge' (as in Pontefract).

Pond from Middle English, meaning a 'dweller by a pond'.

Pont, **Ponte**, **Punt** from Middle English, and Old French, meaning 'someone who lives by the bridge'.

Poor, **Poore**, **Power**, **Powers** from Old French, meaning 'poor'.

Port, **Porte** from Old French, meaning a 'gate' and denoting a gate-keeper.

Porter, **Porters** from Old French, meaning either 'gate-keeper', or one who 'carries baggage/burdens'.

Portman from Old English, meaning a 'town burgess'.

Portnoy, **Portner** from Old French, meaning 'carry night'.

Postle from Old French, meaning 'apostle'.

Pothecary from Old French, meaning 'apothecary', 'keeper of a drug store'.

Pott, **Pot**, **Potts** from Old English, meaning a 'hole/pit' or a diminutive form of 'Philip'.

Potter from Old English, meaning a 'maker of pots'.

Pottenger, **Pottinger** either from Old French, meaning a 'maker/seller of soup', or from Scots Gaelic, meaning an 'apothecary'.

Poulter from Old French, meaning a 'keeper/seller of poultry'.

Pound, **Pounder**, **Pounds** from Old English, meaning an 'enclosure' and denoting someone who lived or worked near a pound.

Powell, **Poel** from Welsh 'ap Howel' meaning 'son of Howel', or Old English meaning 'someone who lives by the pool'.

Poyser, **Poyzer** from Old French, meaning a 'weigher' and denoting someone in charge of the scales/weighing machine.

Pratt, **Pritt** from Old English, meaning a 'trick' or 'cunning, crafty' and therefore possibly denoting a conman.

Pray from Old French, meaning a 'meadow'.

Preece, **Prees** either from Old French meaning 'of the meadows', or from Welsh 'ap Rhys' – 'son of Rhys'.

Prentice, **Prentis**, **Prentiss** from Middle English, meaning an 'apprentice'.

Prescot, **Prescott**, **Priscott** from Old English, meaning a 'priest's house'.

Press, **Prest** *see* **Priest**.

Pressick, **Prestwich**, from Old English, meaning a 'priest's dairy'.

Prestbury from Old English, meaning a 'priest's place'.

Pretty from Old English, meaning 'someone who is clever/crafty'.

Prettyman from Old English, meaning a 'servant of Pretty'.

Price, **Pryse** meaning 'son of Rhys'.

Pride, **Pryde** from Middle English, meaning 'pride'.

Priest, **Prest**, **Press** from Old English, meaning a 'priest'.

Priestley, **Priestly**, **Presley**, **Prisley** from Old English, meaning 'someone who lives near the priest's wood'.

Priestman, **Presman** from Old English, meaning a 'servant of the priest'.

Pritchard, **Prichard**, **Prichards** from Welsh 'ap Richard' meaning 'son of Richard'.

Probert from Welsh 'ap Robert' meaning 'son of Robert'.

Procter from Latin meaning a 'manager/tithe collector'.

Prophet, **Proffitt** from Old French, meaning a 'prophet'.

Proud, **Proude** from Old English, meaning 'someone arrogant'. Hence **Proudfoot** 'someone who walks in an arrogant fashion'.

Proust, **Provis**, **Provost** from Middle English, meaning a 'provost/ steward'.

Prowse, **Prouse** from Middle English, meaning 'valiant'.

Puddifoot, **Pudifoot**, **Puddefoot** from Old English, 'something that is swollen like a pudding' probably denoting a fat man.

Pullan, **Pullen**, **Pullin** probably from Old English, meaning a 'dweller by a pool'.

Pumfrey, **Pumphrey**, **Pomfrey** either from Welsh 'ap Humphrey', 'son of Humphrey', or a form of **Pomfret** (*see p.112*).

Purcell from Old French, meaning a 'little pig/piglet'.

Purley from Old English, meaning a 'field with pear trees'.

Purser from Old English, meaning a 'purse' and denoting a 'maker/ seller of purses'.

Purves, **Purvis** from Old French, meaning 'provider of supplies'.

Pusey from Old English, meaning an 'island/place where peas grow'.

Putnam, **Puttnam** from Old English, meaning a 'farm' village/ dwelling-place by a pit or hollow', denoting someone who lives in such a place.

Pyatt from Old French, meaning a 'magpie'.

Quaif, **Quaife** from Old French, meaning a 'close-fitting cap/skullcap' and referring to a maker/seller of skullcaps.

Quail, **Quaile**, **Quayle** either a Manx form of MacFail, meaning 'son of Paul', or from Old French, meaning 'quail' (a bird known for its amorous, and timorous, nature).

Quainton, **Quinton** from Old English, meaning 'queen's manor house'.

Quant from Old French, meaning 'clever/skilled/crafty'.

Quantrell, **Quantrill** from Old French, meaning a 'dandy/beau'.

Quarrell from Old French, meaning a 'crossbow' and referring to a maker or user of this weapon.

Quarrie, **Quarrier**, **Quarry** from Old French, meaning a 'quarry' and referring to someone who worked in one.

Quartermanin, **Quartermaine**, **Quarterman** from Old French, meaning 'four hands', as in one who wore armour over his hands, or possibly a nickname for someone who was extremely agile.

Queen from Old English, meaning 'queen' and referring to someone who acted like royalty or perhaps to one who served in a royal household.

Quenell, **Quennell**, **Quinnell** from Old English, meaning a 'queen of war'.

Quested from Old English, meaning a 'location next to a wharf'.

Quick, **Quicke**, **Quickly** from Old English, meaning 'quick/swift'.

Quiller from Old French, meaning 'someone who made spoons', or possibly 'someone who quilled or made ruffs'.

Quilter from Old French, meaning 'someone who made or sold quilts/mattresses etc'.

Quincy, **Quincey** probably from the place Cuinchy in Pas-de-Calais, France, but later names could also have come with immigrants from two places called Quincy in France.

Quirk, **Quirke** from the Manx form of MacCorc, meaning 'son of Corc' ('heart').

Rabbatts, **Rabbets**, **Rabbetts**, **Rabbits**, **Rabbit** all arising from the name 'Robert'.

Raby from Old Norse, and Middle English, meaning a 'farm located on a boundary'.

Radcliff, **Radcliffe**, **Ratcliff**, **Ratcliffe**, **Redcliff**, **Redcliffe** from Old English, meaning a 'red cliff' and applied to someone who lived close by.

Radbourne, **Radburn**, **Redbourn**, **Redburn** from Old English, meaning a 'stream with reeds', or a 'red stream' (possibly one with reddish soil and stones at the bottom and/or banks).

Radbone *see* **Rathbone**.

Raddon from Old English, meaning a 'red hill' (owing to the colour of the soil). Similarly, **Radleigh**, **Radley** would be 'someone who lives near a red clearing'; **Radway**, **Reddaway**, **Rodway** a 'dweller near a roadway or red road', and **Radwell** 'someone who lives by a red stream'.

Radford from Old English, meaning a 'red ford' or occasionally a 'reedy ford'.

Rae a Scottish form of **Roe**.

Rain, **Raine**, **Rayne** there are several different meanings attached to this name. It could come from one of two Old French words meaning either 'frog' or 'queen', or it could come from Old German, meaning 'powerful'.

Rainer, Rayner, Raynor, Reiner, Reyner from Old German, meaning a 'counsel/mighty army'.

Rake, Raikes from the Old English word for 'throat' and probably referring to 'someone who lived near a narrow valley/gorge'.

Raleigh, Ralley, Rally, Rawley from Old English, meaning either a 'red clearing' or a 'place populated by roe deer'.

Ralf, Ralfe, Ralph from Old German meaning literally an 'advice wolf'.

Ram, Ramm from Old English, meaning a 'ram' and probably first used as a nickname.

Ramsay, Ramsey from Old English, meaning a 'wild garlic island'.

Ramsbotham, Ramsbottom from Old English, meaning either a 'valley where wild garlic grows' or, more likely, a 'valley with rams'.

Ramshaw *see* **Ravenshaw**.

Randolph from Old Norse, meaning a 'shield wolf'. **Randall, Randell, Randle, Randles, Rankin** are all diminutives of Randolph, while **Ransom** means 'son of Rand(olph)'.

Rank from Old English, and Middle English, meaning a 'strong/proud person'.

Raper from Old English, meaning a 'maker/seller of ropes'.

Rapson meaning 'son of Robert'. A popular name in the county of Cornwall.

Rash from Middle English, meaning 'at or by the ash tree'.

Rathbone, Radbone, Rathborne, Rathbourn this is a name whose origin is obscure. Some people have suggested it could come from Irish, meaning a 'white fort' or from Welsh, meaning a 'clearing'. A third, more gruesome, suggestion is that it is from Old English, meaning a 'man who kills with speed'.

Ratter from Old French, meaning a 'person who catches rats/vermin'.

Rattray from Scots Gaelic, meaning a 'circular fort'.

Raven, **Ravens**, **Revan**, **Revans** from Old English, meaning a 'raven'. Other Raven-related surnames include **Raven(s)hill**, meaning 'someone who lives on a hill with ravens'; **Ravensdale** 'someone who lives in a valley of ravens'; **Ravenshaw**, **Ramshaw**, **Renshaw** 'someone who lives near a raven wood'.

Raw, **Rawe** from Old English, meaning a 'row' and applied to anyone who lived in a row of houses.

Rawdon from Old English, meaning a 'rough hill'.

Rawkins meaning 'little Ralph'.

Ray, **Raye**, **Rey** either from Old French, meaning a 'king' and probably first used as a nickname to denote someone who was very proud, or from Old English, meaning a 'roe deer'.

Raydon from Old English, meaning a 'hill upon which rye grows'.

Rayleigh from Old English, meaning a 'field sown with rye'.

Raymond from Old German meaning 'protector'.

Read, **Reade**, **Reed**, **Reid** from Old English, meaning 'red' and probably referring to someone with a red face or red hair. However, if it derives from Middle English, it can mean a 'reed bed'.

Reader from Old English, meaning 'someone who works with reeds' i.e. a thatcher/craftsman.

Readett, **Readitt** from Old English, meaning 'someone who lives by the reed beds'.

Reading, **Redding**, **Riding** from Old English, meaning a 'clearing'.

Ready, **Readey**, **Readdy**, **Reddie** from Middle English, meaning 'someone prepared for action/quick/up to speed'.

Reagan, **Regan** from Irish O'Regan, meaning 'descendant of Riagán' ('little king').

Reaper from Old English, meaning a 'reaper'.

Reddish, Redditch, Redish from Old English, meaning a 'reedy place/ditch/fen'.

Redfern, Redfearn from Old English, meaning a 'red species of bracken/fern'.

Redhead, Readhead from Old English, meaning 'someone with red hair'.

Redmond an Irish form of 'Raymond'.

Reeve from Old English, meaning a 'reeve/bailiff'.

Reeves from Old English, meaning a 'servant in the house of a bailiff/magistrate'.

Reid a Scots form of 'Read' and a common name in Scotland.

Reilly from Irish 'O'Reilly', meaning a 'descendant of Valiant'.

Remfrey, Remfry, Renfree from Old German, meaning 'might peace'.

Renner from Old English, meaning a 'runner' and probably applied to messengers/heralds.

Revel, Revell, Revill from Latin and Old French, meaning a 'rebel/rebellion/insolent,' etc.

Revere from Old English, meaning 'someone who lives on the brow of a hill'.

Reynard, Renhard from Old French and Old German, meaning 'counsel-brave'.

Reynold, Reynolds, Reynalds from Old German meaning 'counsel power/might.'

Rhys, Reece, Rice from Old Welsh meaning 'ardour' and applied to those with an amorous nature.

Ricard *see* **Richard**.

Rich, Riche from Middle English, meaning 'rich', but can also be a diminutive of the name 'Richard', or from Old English, meaning a 'dweller by a stream'.

Richard, **Richardes**, **Richards**, **Ritchard**, **Ricard**, **Rickards**, **Rickard** from Old German, meaning 'powerful/brave'. This was one of the most popular names introduced to Britain by the Normans. It has spawned a large number of surnames: **Richey**, **Richie**, **Rick**, **Ricks**, **Rix**, **Ritchie** are all diminutives, while **Rickman** means a 'servant of Rick/Richard'. Many have also been made into patronyms. (*See also* **Dick**.)

Richmond, **Richmont** from Old French, meaning a 'fine or splendid hill'.

Rickward, **Rickword**, **Rickwood** from Old German, meaning a 'powerful guardian'.

Riddell, **Riddle**, **Riddall**, **Riddle**, **Riddles** from Old French, meaning a 'small hill' and probably applied to someone who dwelt near/on one.

Ride, **Ryde** from Old English, meaning a 'dweller in a clearing'.

Rider from Old English, meaning a 'rider' and probably referring to a knight or cavalryman.

Ridge from Old English, meaning 'one who lives on a ridge', hence **Ridgeway** would be 'one who lives on a ridgeway/ridge road'.

Ridler from Old English, meaning a 'sieve' and either denoting a 'sieve maker' or referring to someone who sieved corn/sand, etc.

Rigby from Old Norse, meaning 'someone who lives on or near a farm on a ridge'.

Rigg, **Rigge**, **Riggs** from Old Norse, meaning 'someone who lives on a ridge'.

Riley, **Ryley** from Old English, meaning a 'clearing with rye'.

Rimer, **Rimmer**, **Rymer** from Middle English, meaning 'to rhyme' and applied to a poet.

Ring, **Ringe**, **Rings** from Old English, meaning a 'ring' and probably referring to a maker/seller of rings/jewellery.

Ringer from Old English, meaning a 'bell-ringer'.

Ringwood from Old English, meaning a 'border wood/copse'.

Riordan from Irish O'Riordan, meaning a 'descendant of Royal Bard'.

Ripper from Old Norse, meaning a 'weaver of baskets/a basket seller'.

Risby from Old Norse, meaning a 'dweller at the farm by the clearing'.

Rise, **Risely** from Old English, meaning 'someone who lives near a brushwood'.

Rivers from Old French, and denoting someone who lived by a river.

Roake, **Roke**, from Middle English, meaning 'at the oak' and denoting someone who lived near one or more oak trees.

Robert, **Roberts**, **Robard**, **Robarts**, **Robberds**, **Robers** from Old German, meaning 'flame bright'. This name has generated many other surnames – as diminutives or patronymics. Among them are **Robb**, **Robbs**, **Robin**, **Robins**, all diminutives and **Robson**, **Robinson**, etc. (*See also* **Dobb**.)

Roch, **Roche**, **Rochelle**, **Rocall** from Old French, meaning a 'rock' or 'place by a rock'.

Rochester, **Rossiter** probably meaning a 'town of bridges/at the bridges'. Rochester is also a town in Kent.

Rockefeller from Old German, meaning a 'rye field' and describing someone who lived close by or worked in one.

Rocker from Old English, meaning 'someone who lives at/near the rock' or from Middle English, meaning a 'distaff' (a stick which holds flax/wool in spinning) and therefore applied to a maker of distaffs.

Rodd from Old English, meaning a 'clearing'.

Roe from Old English, meaning a 'roe deer'.

Roger, **Rogers**, **Rodger**, **Rodgers** from Old German, meaning a 'fame spear'. Pet forms of this name include Hodge and Dodge.

Rock, Rocke, Rocks probably from Middle English, meaning 'rock' and indicating a person who dwelt on or by a rock, or possibly meaning 'at the oak' and denoting someone who lived near an oak tree.

Roland, Rolland, Rolands, Rowland from Old German, meaning 'famous land'.

Rolf, Rolfe, Rolph, Ruff from Old German, meaning a 'fame wolf'.

Romer, Roomer, Rummer from Middle English, meaning a 'person who has made a pilgrimage to Rome'.

Ronald a Scots form of 'Reynold'.

Rook, Rooke, Rookes, Rooks from Old English, meaning a 'rook' and probably begun as a nickname.

Roosevelt from Dutch 'Van Rosevelt' meaning 'of the rose field'.

Root, Roote, Rootes, Roots from Old English, meaning a 'glad/happy person'.

Roper, Raper, Rapier from Old English, meaning a 'maker/seller of ropes'.

Rose, Royce, Royse there are various different meanings applied to this name. It can come from Old German, meaning 'fame-kind'; from Middle English, meaning a 'rose', or from Scots Gaelic, meaning a 'promontory or headland'.

Ross the most likely source of this name is (like Rose) Scots Gaelic, meaning a 'headland/promontory'.

Roth from Old English, meaning 'someone who lives in a clearing'.

Round, Rounds from Old French, meaning 'someone who is round/fat'.

Rous, Rouse, Rowse, Russ from Middle English, and Old French, meaning 'red' and applied to those people with a red complexion or red hair.

Rover from Old English, meaning a 'roofer'.

Rowan from Old Norse, meaning a 'rowan bush, mountain ash'.

Row, **Rowe** from Old English, meaning a 'row' and probably applied to someone who lived in a row of cottages/houses or by a hedgerow.

Rower from Old French, meaning a 'wheelwright'.

Rowley from Old English, meaning a 'clearing in a wood'.

Rowney from Old English, meaning 'someone who lives near a rough enclosure'.

Rowntree from Old Norse, meaning a 'rowan bush/tree/mountain ash'.

Roy from Old French, meaning a 'king'.

Royal, **Royle** from Old English, meaning a 'hill with a crop of rye growing upon it'.

Rubinstein meaning a 'ruby stone'.

Rudd from Old English, meaning 'ruddy'. Hence **Rudkin**, **Rudman** meaning a 'ruddy/red-haired person'.

Rudge from Old English, and Middle English, meaning 'someone who lives on or by a ridge'.

Rumbellow, **Rumbelow** from Old English, meaning a 'person who lives by the three hills/burrows'.

Runcie from Middle English, meaning an 'old riding-horse/nag'.

Runciman from Middle English, meaning 'someone who looks after the rouncies/old nags'.

Rundall, **Rundell**, **Rundle** from Old French, meaning 'rotund/plump'.

Rush from Old English, meaning 'rushes'.

Rusher from Old English, meaning a 'cutter/seller of rushes'.

Rushton from Old English, meaning a 'farm/house located in or by rushes'.

Russel, Russell, Rousel, Rousell from Old French, meaning a 'red-haired/faced person' (*see* **Rous**).

Rust from Old English, meaning 'with red hair or a red face'.

Rutter either from Old French, meaning 'someone who played the rote' (a stringed musical instrument) or from another Old French word meaning a 'highwayman/ruffian'.

Ryan from the Irish O'Ryan, very common in County Tipperary, but of uncertain origin and meaning.

Rydell from Old English, meaning a 'valley in which rye grows'.

Ryman from Old English, meaning 'someone who lives on low-lying land'.

Sach, **Sacher**, **Sack**, **Sacker**, **Sachs**, **Secker** from Old French, meaning a 'maker/seller of sackcloth/sacks'.

Saddler, **Sadler** from Old English, meaning a 'maker/seller of saddles'.

Sagar, **Sager** from Old English, meaning a 'sea spear'.

Sage from Old French, meaning 'wise'.

Sailer, **Saylor**, **Seyler** from Old French, meaning a 'dancer'.

Sainsbury possibly from Old English, meaning a 'sea friend's fort', possibly indicating from 'a fort/town named after a saint'.

Saint from Old French, meaning a 'saint' and no doubt begun as a nickname for someone who was conspicuously virtuous.

Salaman, **Salamon**, **Salamons**, **Salomon**, **Salomons**, **Salman**, **Salmen**, **Salmon**, **Salmond**, **Salmons** most often from Hebrew *shalom* meaning 'peace' but occasionally from Old English, and Middle English, meaning a 'salesman'. There is absolutely no connection whatsoever with the fish.

Salingar, **Salinger**, **Seliger**, **Selinger**, **Sellinger** probably from the French town of Saint-Léger.

Salley from Old English, meaning a 'sallow clearing'.

Salter, **Sauter**, **Sawter** can either be from Old English, meaning a 'worker in a salt pit' or a 'seller of salt', or it can come from Old French, meaning 'one who played the psaltery' (a type of harp).

Saltern, **Salterne** from Old English, meaning 'someone who worked at the salthouse'.

Sam, **Samms**, **Sams** a diminutive form of 'Samson'.

Sambourn, **Sambourne** from Old English, meaning a 'sandy stream'.

Sample *see* **Semple**.

Sampson, **Samson**, can be traced back to the biblical Samson meaning 'son of Shamash'. Also believed to come from the French town Saint-Samson.

Samuel, **Samuels** from Hebrew, meaning 'name of God'. As a surname it is not solely of Jewish origin.

Samways from Old English, meaning 'foolish'.

Sand, **Sandes**, **Sands**, **Sandys** from Old English, meaning 'sand' and applied to someone who lived by sands or on sandy earth.

Sandars, **Sander**, **Sanders**, **Saunder**, **Saunders** probably a pet form of 'Alexander'.

Sandell, **Sandells** from Old English, meaning 'someone who lives by a sandy hill/slope'.

Sandeman from Old English, meaning a 'servant of Saunder' ('Alexander').

Sandford from Old English, meaning 'someone who lives by a sandy ford'.

Sangar, **Sanger** from Old English, meaning a 'singer' and probably denoting a chorister.

Santer *see* **Senter**.

Sapper from Old English, meaning 'someone who makes/sells soap'.

Sargant, **Sargeant**, **Sargent**, **Seargeant**, **Seargant**, **Sergent** from Old French, meaning a 'servant' or 'a court officer' or 'someone in military service below the rank of knight'.

Sarson, **Sarsons** meaning a 'son of Sara' or a 'Saracen' (a Syrian or Arab nomad). When the Crusaders returned from abroad they brought back a number of Saracen captives as servants.

Satchel, **Satchell** from Old French, meaning a 'little bag' and applied to a maker/seller of these.

Savage from Old French and Latin, meaning 'someone who was savage/wild/unkempt'.

Sawers from Old English, meaning 'a sower' (of seeds).

Sawyer, **Sawyers** from Middle English, meaning 'to saw' and applied to those who sawed wood or timber.

Saxby, **Shakesby** from Old Norse and Old French, meaning 'draw sword'.

Saxon from Old German, meaning a 'Saxon' ('German people of the knife/short sword').

Sayer, **Sayers**, **Seyers**, **Sear**, **Seares**, **Sears**, **Seers** there are several different interpretations to this name. It may come from Old English 'to say' and be applied to a reciter/storyteller. Or it may be from Old French, meaning 'someone who tests things' and be applied to a food-taster. Or it might come from another Old French word meaning 'silk/serge' and refer to a maker or seller of silk.

Scale, **Scales** from Old Norse and Middle English, meaning 'someone who dwells by a hut'.

Scarf, **Scarfe**, **Scarffe** from Old Norse, meaning a 'cormorant'.

Scargill from Old Norse, meaning a 'ravine with mergansers' (a species of large diving duck, although Latin *anser* actually means 'goose').

Scarlet, **Scarlett** from Old French, meaning 'scarlet'. Scarlet was the name of a particular cloth and so the name probably refers to a dealer in scarlet.

Scatchard from Old Norse and Old French, meaning a 'maker of stilts'.

Schlesinger of German origin meaning someone from Silesia or Schleusingen in Thuringia.

Schofield, **Scholdfield**, **Scolfield**, **Scoffield**, **Scofield** from Old Norse and Old English, meaning 'someone who lives by a field with a hut'.

Scholar, **Scoular**, **Scouler** from Old Norse, meaning 'someone who lives in the shieling' (shelter or hut or, sometimes, cattle pasture).

Scorer from Old French, meaning either a 'scourer/cleaner' or a 'scout', or from Old English, meaning 'someone who lives on a steep hillside'.

Scott, **Scotts** from Old English, meaning originally 'an Irishman' but then later on it came to mean a 'Gael from Scotland'. On occasion the name might also come from the personal name 'Scott'. Whatever the case, this is a very common surname on both sides of the English/Scottish border.

Scriminger Scrimshaw, **Skrimshaw** from Old French, meaning a 'fencing master'.

Scriven, **Scrivens**, **Scrivener**, **Scrivenor** from Old French, meaning a 'writer/copier/scribe'.

Scudamore *see* **Skidmore**.

Seaberg, **Siberg** from Old English, meaning a 'sea fortress/castle'.

Seabert, **Seabright**, **Sebright** from Old English, meaning 'sea bright'.

Seagram from Old English and Middle English, meaning a 'servant', but probably applied to a sailor.

Seal, **Seale**, **Seales** from Old English, meaning a 'hall' and applied to someone who lived at the hall, that is the manor or great house.

Sealey, **Seely**, **Selly**, **Silly**, **Cely**, from Old English, meaning 'blessed'.

Seaman, **Seamons**, **Seman**, **Semens** from Old English, meaning a 'seaman/sailor'.

Sear, Seare, Seares, Sears *see* **Sayer.**

Searl, Searle, Searles, Searls from Old German, meaning 'armour'.

Seaton, Seton from Old English, meaning a 'place by the sea' or a 'dweller on cultivated land'.

Secker from Old English, meaning a 'maker/seller of sackcloth' (*see also* **Sack**).

Sedge from Old English, meaning 'sedge, reed' and referring to someone who lived in a sedgy spot. Other sedgy names are **Sedgeman** meaning 'someone who works with sedge' i.e. a thatcher of roofs; **Sedgemoor, Sedgemore** 'someone who lives near/on a moor with sedge'; **Sedgewick, Sedgwick, Sedgewicke, Sidgewick** meaning 'someone who lives on a dairy farm in the sedge'.

Seers *see* **Sayer.**

Selborne, Selbourne from Old English, meaning a 'stream in the willow trees'.

Selden, Seldon from Old English, meaning a 'house on a hill'.

Self, Selfe from Old English, meaning a 'sea wolf'.

Sell, Selle from Old English, meaning a 'shelter for animals' or 'herdsman's hut'.

Sellar, Sellars, Seller, Sellers, Sellors, Zeller either from Old French, meaning a 'maker/seller of saddles', or from Middle English, meaning 'to give' and therefore denoting a 'seller of goods, a dealer/tradesman'.

Sellerman from Old English, meaning 'someone who works in a cellar'.

Sellman, Selman from Old English, meaning a 'happy/content man'.

Selwin, Selwyn from Latin meaning 'of the woods' and probably referring to a woodsman.

Semple, Sempill, Sample from the French place name 'Saint-Paul'.

Senior either from Old French, meaning 'lord' (of the manor) or from Latin meaning 'older' and therefore 'senior' in rank.

Senter, **Sainter**, **Santer** from Old French, meaning a 'maker of bells'.

Servant, **Servent** from Old French, meaning a 'servant' or 'sergeant'.

Sessions from the city of Soissons in France.

Seton *see* **Seaton**.

Setter, **Setters** most likely from Old English, meaning 'to set' and applied to a bricklayer or stonemason.

Sewal, **Sewall**, **Sewell** from Old English, meaning 'sea power/guard/ruler'.

Seward, **Sewards**, **Sewart** from Old English, meaning a 'sea victory' or occasionally from another Old English word meaning a 'sow-herd'.

Sexton, **Sexon** from Old French, meaning 'sacristan', itself a less common word for a sexton, the person who looked after the contents of a church.

Seymour, **Seymore**, **Seymer** from the French town 'Saint-Maur'.

Shackleton a Scandinavianized form of Old English, meaning 'farm on a tongue of land'.

Shade from Old English and Middle English, meaning a 'shadow' and probably referring to a very thin man. It may in some instances mean 'boundary'.

Shakesby *see* **Saxby**.

Shakeshaft from Old English, meaning one who 'shakes or brandishes a shaft or spear', a spearman.

Shakespeare, **Shakespear** from Old English, with the same meaning as **Shakeshaft** (*above*), and the most famous surname in the language.

Shank, **Shanks** from Old English, meaning 'shank, leg', a nickname for a person whose legs must have been his most noticeable feature.

Shapcott from Old English, meaning a 'sheep shed'.

Shard, **Sheard** from Old English, meaning 'someone who lives by a cleft in a hill'.

Sharman, **Shearman**, **Sheerman**, **Sherman** from Old English, meaning a 'shearman' i.e. someone who shears cloth to remove the nap. **Shearer** has the same meaning.

Sharp, **Sharpe** from Old English, meaning 'sharp/clever/quick'.

Sharples most likely from Old English, meaning a 'high pasture/ field'.

Shaw, **Shawe** from Old English, meaning a 'dweller by a wood/ copse'.

Shawcross from Old English, meaning 'someone who lives by the cross in the wood'.

Shearsmith from Old English, meaning a 'maker/seller of scissors'.

Sheather from Old English, meaning a 'maker/seller of sheaths for swords'.

Sheehan from Irish O'Sheehan, meaning a 'descendant of Peaceful'.

Sheen from Old English, meaning 'someone who lives by a hut/shed'.

Sheerman *see* **Sharman**.

Sheepshanks from Old English, meaning 'sheep legs' and probably first used as a nickname for someone with legs like those of a sheep.

Sheer, **Sheere** from Old English, meaning 'bright/fair'.

Shefford from Old English, meaning 'someone who lives by the sheep ford'.

Sheldon from Old English, meaning 'someone who lives by the steep-sided valley/gorge'.

Sheldrake from Old English, meaning 'sheldrake' (of the duck family).

Shelton, **Shilton** from Old English, meaning 'someone who lives by a place on a bank'.

Shepard, **Shepeard**, **Shephard**, **Shepheard**, **Shepherd**, **Sheppard**, **Shepperd**, **Shepherd**, **Shippard** from Old English, meaning a 'shepherd'.

Sheppey from Old English, for someone who lives on an 'island with sheep'.

Sherborn, **Sherborne**, **Sherbourn**, **Sherbourne** from Old English, meaning someone who lives by the 'bright stream'. Similarly derived are names such as **Shergold** meaning 'bright gold'; **Sherlock** meaning 'bright/fair/shining' and no doubt applied to someone with fair hair; **Sherrard**, **Sherrad**, **Sheratt** meaning 'bright-hard', and **Sherwood** meaning a 'bright wood' and applied to someone who lived close by. Alternatively the latter name could also mean a 'wood belonging to the shire'.

Sheriff from Old English, meaning 'an officer of the law/sheriff'.

Sherwin from Old English, meaning 'to cut the wind' and no doubt applied to a swift runner.

Shield, **Shields** from Old English, may mean a 'shield' and have been applied to a maker/seller of shields, or it may come from the word for 'shed/shelter' and have been applied to someone living by one.

Shingler from Middle English, meaning 'to use/cover with shingles' and applied to a roofer.

Shipley from Old English, meaning a 'pasture with sheep'.

Shipman from Old English, meaning either a 'sailor' or a 'shepherd' (a sheep-man).

Shipton from Old English, meaning a 'sheep farm'.

Shipwright from Old English, meaning just that – someone who builds ships.

Shooter, **Shotter** from Old English, meaning 'someone who shoots' and perhaps applied to an archer.

Shore, **Shores** from Middle English, meaning 'someone who lives by the shore'.

Shufflebottom from Old English, meaning 'someone who lives in or by the sheep-fell valley'.

Sibley, **Sibly** from Greek and Latin, meaning 'Sibyl' (a woman acting as a mouth-piece for the gods).

Siddall, **Siddel**, **Siddell** from Old English, meaning a 'hill-side'.

Side from Old English, meaning 'someone who lives by a slope'.

Sidebotham, **Sidebottom** from Old English, meaning a 'broad valley' and denoting someone who lived in or near one.

Sidney, **Sydney** from Old English, meaning 'someone who lives by the wide or well watered land/island'. Some people believe that the name could be derived from the French town of Saint-Denis in Normandy but this has yet to be proved.

Sievewright from Old English, meaning 'someone who makes/sells sieves'.

Siggers, **Siger** from Old English, meaning a 'victory spear'.

Silcock, **Silcox** a diminutive form of 'Silvester' plus 'cock' or 'cox'.

Silk from Old English, meaning a 'maker/seller of silk'.

Sillitoe, **Shillito**, **Shileto** a Yorkshire name of unknown origin or meaning.

Silver from Old English, meaning 'silver' and most likely applied to a 'silversmith'.

Silvester, **Sylvester** from Latin meaning 'someone who lives in a forest'.

Sim, **Simm**, **Simms**, **Sims** a diminutive form of 'Simon'. **Simcock**, **Simcocks** is the same diminutive plus 'cock' or 'cox'. Other diminutives include **Simkin**, **Simkins**, **Simpkin**, **Simpkins**.

Simon, **Simeon** from Hebrew, meaning 'hearkening', or from the Greek, meaning 'snub-nosed'. Variants include **Simmonds**,

Simmons, Symmons and **Simond, Symond. Simonson, Simison** mean 'son of Simon', as does **Simpson; Simpkinson** is 'son of Simpkin'.

Simple from Old French, meaning 'simple, honest, open'.

Sinclair, Sinclaire, St Clair this name originates from the French town of Saint-Clair in La Manche and perhaps from Latin, meaning 'bright/shining'.

Singer, Singers from Old English, meaning a 'singer'.

Singleton from Old English, meaning 'someone who lives by a shingle-roofed farm'.

Sinnatt, Sinnett, Sinnott from Old English, meaning 'victory bold'.

Sisley, Sicley from Latin *Caecilia,* which stems from *caecus* meaning 'blind', the name of St Cecilia who was the patron saint of music. The Normans introduced this name into England and it soon became very popular.

Sisson, Sissons meaning a 'son of Sisley'.

Sixsmith from Old English, meaning a 'maker of scythes'.

Sizer from Middle English, meaning an 'assizer/sworn witness'.

Skeat, Skeats from Old Norse, meaning 'swift of foot'.

Skegg, Skeggs from Old Norse, meaning a 'bearded man'.

Skelton from Old English, meaning 'someone who lives on a hill'.

Skepper from Old Norse, meaning a 'maker/seller of baskets'.

Skidmore, Scudamore from Old English, meaning a 'person who lives by a muddy moor/field'.

Slack either from Old English, meaning 'someone who is lazy' or from Old Norse, meaning 'someone who lives in a shallow valley or gorge'.

Slade, Slader from Old English, meaning 'someone who lives in a valley'.

Slater, Slator, Slatter from Middle English, meaning 'slate' and probably referring to someone who made or repaired roofs.

Slaughter either from Old English, meaning a 'muddy place/a slough', or from Middle English, meaning 'to slaughter' and therefore referring to a 'slaughterer of livestock' i.e. a butcher.

Slay either from Old Norse, meaning 'sly/cunning', or from Middle English, meaning 'a tool used in weaving' and, like **Slaymaker**, probably denoting a maker of these.

Slayter, Slaytor from Old English, meaning 'slaughter' and therefore a butcher.

Slocomb, Slocombe most likely from Old English, meaning 'someone who dwells by a valley where sloes grow'.

Sloper from Middle English, meaning a 'maker/seller of tunics'.

Smail, Smailes from Old English, meaning 'someone who lives by a burrow'.

Smale, Smales, Small from Old English, meaning 'thin, slender'.

Smallbone, Smallbones from Old English, meaning 'someone with slender bones'.

Smallbridge from Old English, meaning 'someone who lives by the narrow bridge'.

Smallcombe from Old English, meaning 'someone who lives by the narrow valley'.

Smallpeace, Smallpiece from Old English, meaning 'someone who lives by the narrow strip of land'.

Smallwood from Old English, meaning 'someone who lives by the narrow wood'.

Smart from Old English, meaning 'quick/prompt'.

Smedley from Old English, meaning 'someone who lives by a flat clearing'.

Smith, Smithe, Smyth, Smythe from Old English, meaning a 'blacksmith/farrier/metal-worker' although occasionally it can also mean 'someone who lived near a smeeth' or plain. Smith is widely thought to be the commonest surname in the British Isles and in the USA.

Smithers from Old English, meaning a 'hammerman, smith'.

Smitherman from Old English, meaning 'someone who works at the smithy'.

Smollett from Old English, meaning 'someone with a small head'.

Snape from Old English, meaning 'someone who lives by the pasture/field'.

Snead, **Sneed**, **Snoad** from Old English, meaning a 'clearing in a wood' and applied to someone who lived nearby.

Snel, **Snell**, **Snelles** from Old English, meaning 'clever/bold'.

Snelgar from Old English, meaning a 'bold spear'.

Snider, **Sniders** from Old English, meaning 'to cut' and probably denoting a cutter of cloth/a tailor.

Snook, **Snooks** from Old English, meaning 'pointed' and perhaps referring to a piece of land.

Snow from Old English, meaning just that, and applied to someone with white hair or to someone who was born or baptized during snow.

Snowden, **Snowdon** from Old English, meaning a 'hill with snow'.

Soame, **Soames** from Old English, meaning a 'homestead near water'.

Soan, **Soane** from Old English, meaning 'son'.

Soaper, **Soper** from Old English, meaning a 'maker/seller of soap'.

Soar, **Soares** from Old French, meaning a 'reddish-brown colour' and probably referring to a person's hair.

Somers, **Somersfield**, etc. *see* **Summerby**, etc.

Sorbie, **Sorby**, **Sowerby** from Old Norse, meaning a 'muddy farm'.

Sorrel, **Sorrell** from Old French, meaning a 'reddish-brown colour'.

Sotheby from Old Norse, denoting 'someone who lived in the south part of the village'.

Sotheran, **Sothern**, **Southan**, **Southern** from Old English, meaning 'southern' and denoting someone from the south. Among other southerly surnames are **Southam** for someone who dwelt on a 'farm in the south'; **Southcomb**, **Southcombe** for a person who lived in a 'south valley'; **Southgate** from Old English, for someone who lived by the 'south gate'; **Southwell** for one who lived by the 'south spring, stream or well'; **Southwood** for someone who lived by the 'south wood', and **Sowman** from Old English, denoting a 'man from the south'.

Soutar, **Souter**, **Soutter** from Old English, meaning a 'shoemaker'.

Sowden from Old French, meaning a 'sultan' and probably started as a nickname.

Spark, **Sparke**, **Sparkes**, **Sparks** from Old Norse, meaning 'bright/lively'.

Speak, **Speake**, **Speaks**, **Speaight**, **Speight** from Old French, meaning a 'woodpecker'.

Speakman from Middle English, meaning a 'spokesman'.

Spear, **Speare**, **Speares**, **Spears**, **Speers**, **Speers** from Old English, meaning a 'spear' and probably denoting a foot soldier, a spearman.

Speed from Old English, meaning 'wealth, success'.

Speight *see* **Speak**.

Spier, **Spiers**, **Speir**, **Speirs** from Old French, meaning a 'spy/someone who watches'.

Spellar, **Speller** from Old English, meaning a 'narrator, a preacher'.

Spence, **Spens** from Old French, meaning a 'larder/buttery' – a place from where provisions were dispensed – and denoting someone who was in charge of one, a steward or butler. **Spencer,** **Spenser** have the same meaning.

Spender from Old French, meaning, like **Spencer** (*above*), a 'steward'.

Spicer from Old French, meaning 'someone who deals in/sells spices'.

Spiller, Spillman from Old English, meaning a 'fool/jester'.

Spindler from Old English, meaning a 'spindle' and denoting a 'maker of spindles'.

Spink, Spinks from Middle English, meaning a 'finch'.

Spinner from Old English, meaning a 'spinner' (of yarn).

Spital, Spittal, Spittall, Spittle, Spittler from Middle English, meaning a 'hospital' and denoting someone who worked in one.

Spooner from Old English, meaning a 'splinter' and probably denoting someone who repaired roofs with shingle.

Spray, Sprey from Middle English, meaning a 'slim twig' and probably alluding to someone who was very thin.

Spring from Middle English, meaning 'the season of spring' and probably denoting someone born or christened during this time.

Springer from Old English, meaning 'someone who was lively/quick'.

Sproat, Sprot from Old English, meaning a 'shoot, twig' and possibly referring to a young person.

Spurr from Old English, meaning a 'spur' and probably denoting a 'spurrier', as do **Spurrier, Spurren, Sperrin, Spearon.**

Squiller from Old French, meaning 'someone who makes/sells dishes' or a 'someone who works in a scullery'.

Squire, Squires from Middle English, meaning an 'esquire/shield bearer'.

Squirrel, Squirrell from Old French, meaning a 'squirrel' and perhaps describing someone who was a good climber of hills etc. or a hoarder.

Stable, **Stables** from Old French, but with two modern English meanings – thus probably denoting the man in charge of a stable, or it may mean someone who was steady and reliable.

Stack from Old Norse, meaning a 'heap/haystack', either a name for a builder of haystacks, or a nickname for a man built like one.

Stafford from Old English, meaning someone living near 'a ford by a landing position, marked with staves'.

Stagg from Old English, meaning a 'stag'.

Stain, **Staine**, **Staines** *see* **Stein**.

Stainer, **Steiner** from Middle English, meaning a 'stainer' and probably referring to a painter or someone working with stained glass.

Stainfield from Old English, meaning a 'dweller by a field of stones'.

Stalker from Old English and Middle English, meaning 'someone who walks with stealth'.

Stallwood, **Stallworthy** from Old English, meaning 'robust/sturdy'.

Stamp, **Stamps** most likely from Étampes in France.

Stamper most probably stemming from Middle English, meaning 'someone who treads grapes' or perhaps referring to someone who 'stamped coins'.

Stanbridge from Old English, meaning a 'dweller by a stone bridge'. Similarly, **Standen** means someone who lives in a 'stony valley'; **Standish** a 'stony field/enclosure'; **Stanhill** a 'stony hill'; **Stanhope** a 'stony valley' again; **Stanley**, **Stanly** a 'stony clearing'; **Stanton**, **Staunton** an 'enclosure built on stony ground', and **Stanway** for someone who lived by a 'stone/stony roadway'.

Staple, **Staples** from Old English, meaning a 'pillar/post'. Hence **Stapleford** meaning a 'ford by a pillar/post', and **Stapleton** for someone who lived on a 'farm by a pillar/post'.

Starbuck from Old Norse, meaning a 'stream/rivulet in sedge'.

Stark, Starke, Starkey, Starkie from Old English, meaning 'stark, bleak, harsh, barren' – for someone who dwelt in such a place.

Starr from Old English, meaning a 'star'.

Start, Starte, Stert, Sterte, Sturt, Sturte from Old English, meaning a 'promontory/ tongue of land/hill spur' and probably denoting someone who lived on one.

Statham from Old English, meaning 'someone who lives at the landing place'.

Stead, Steed from Old English, meaning either a 'farm' and therefore applied to a farmer, or a 'horse/steed', in which case it was probably a nickname for someone of strength and high spirits.

Steadman, Stedman as above – from Old English, meaning either a 'farmer/farm-worker' or a 'horseman/groom'.

Steel, Steele from Old English, meaning 'steel'.

Steer, Steares from Old English, meaning a 'steer'.

Stein, Stain, Staine, Staines and other variants most probably derive from Old Norse/Old Danish/Old HighGerman, meaning 'stone'.

Steiner *see* **Stainer**.

Stephen, Stephens, Steven, Stevens, from Greek, meaning a 'crown/wreath'. This name became very common after the Norman Conquest.

Stert, Sterte *see* **Start**.

Steward, Stewart, Steuart, Stuart from Old English, meaning a 'steward'. Originally one who looked after a family's household, the steward, especially in Scotland, grew in importance to become a very high-ranking official. The final *t* is said to be a Scots introduction, and the *u* spelling was apparently the French spelling popularized by Mary, Queen of Scots.

Stile, Stiles, Styles, Stileman from Old English, meaning 'someone who lives by the stile'.

Stilton from Old English, meaning a 'place with a stile'.

Stirling most likely from the Scottish town of Stirling, which in 1147 was called Strivelin. Otherwise the name might derive from 'Starling'.

Stock, **Stocks** from Old English, meaning a 'tree trunk/stump' or 'stocks'. Hence **Stockbridge** for someone who lived by a 'wooden/log bridge'; **Stockdale** a 'valley of tree stumps'; **Stockford** a 'ford next to the stump'; **Stocking** a 'place/field cleared of tree stumps', and **Stockwell** for 'someone who dwelt near a 'spring by a tree stump'.

Stodart, **Stoddard**, **Stoddart**, **Stuttard** from Old English, meaning a 'stud-farm' and probably referring to a servant in charge of it.

Stokes from Old English, meaning a 'religious place/house'.

Stoller from Old English, meaning 'someone who makes/sells stoles – long scarves or shawls'.

Stone, **Stones** from Old English, meaning a 'stone' and referring to someone who lived by a prominent stone or rock.

Stonebridge from Old English, meaning 'someone who lives by the stone bridge'; likewise **Stonehouse** one who owned or dwelt in a 'stone house', and **Stoneman** for 'someone who works with stone'.

Stopford, **Stopforth**, **Stoppard** the most likely meaning is from Old English, meaning 'a market place in a village/hamlet'.

Storer from Middle English, meaning 'someone who stores things' and perhaps denoting a 'storekeeper'.

Storey, **Story** probably from Old Norse, meaning 'large'.

Storm, **Stormes** from Old English, meaning a 'storm/tempest'.

Storr, **Storrs** from Old Norse, meaning either 'large' or perhaps 'a plantation of young trees'.

Stott from Middle English, meaning a 'bullock', probably a nickname, perhaps for a lively, sturdy young man.

Stout, **Stoute** from Old French, meaning 'someone bold/stout'.

Stow, **Stowe** from Old English, meaning 'someone who lives by a holy site'.

Strachan from Scots Gaelic, meaning 'someone who lives in a small valley'.

Strang a Northern form of the name 'Strong'.

Strange, **Stranger**, **Lestrange** from Old French, meaning a 'stranger/newcomer'.

Strangway, **Strangeways** from Old English, meaning an 'overwhelming force/current of water.'

Stratton, **Stretton** from Old English, meaning a 'place/location on a Roman road'.

Street, **Streete**, **Streat** from Old English, meaning a 'Roman road/street', and like **Streeter**, **Streater** denoting 'someone who lives on a street'.

Stretch from Old English, meaning 'violent/severe'.

String, **Stringer** from Old English, meaning 'string/rope' and applied to a maker/seller of strings for bows.

Stringfellow from Old English and Middle English, meaning a 'strong fellow/friend'.

Strong, **Stronge**, **Strang** from Old English and Middle English, meaning 'strong', therefore meaning, like the names **Strongman**, **Strangman**, 'a strong man'.

Stubbe, **Stubbs** from Old English, meaning a 'stump' and probably referring to a person of small stature. Alternatively it may mean 'someone living near the tree-stump'.

Stubbing, **Stubbings** from Middle English, meaning 'someone who lives on land cleared of trees'.

Stud, **Studds** from Old English, meaning 'someone who lives/works at a stud'.

Studebaker from German, meaning 'one who made or sold pastries'.

Studman from Old English, meaning 'someone who works at a stud'.

Stufflebeem a name that came recently into prominence following the terrorist attacks upon New York and Washington on 11 September 2001. The Pentagon spokesman for the military operations mounted against the terrorist al-Qaeda group and its Taliban supporters in Afghanistan was Rear-Admiral John Dickson Stufflebeem, USN. Its meaning is obscure. If the name is of English origin, it could mean 'narrow-hipped', from Middle English for a horse's narrow hip joint 'stifle', plus 'beam'; alternatively, and perhaps more likely, it is of Germanic origin and might mean a 'rigid, upright tree' (denoting someone living near one or resembling one) or a 'wooden rung or steps/wooden ladder' or a 'wooden building with steps' (a builder who works in wood, maybe).

Sturdy from Old French, meaning someone 'brave/fierce' (in battle).

Sturge, **Sturges**, **Sturgess from** Old Norse, meaning 'Thor's hostage'.

Sturgeon from Old French, meaning a 'sturgeon', a nickname, perhaps for someone thin and bony with a long nose, or someone who caught the fish.

Sturrock from Old English, meaning 'someone who lives by a high rock'.

Sturt, **Sturte** *see* **Start**.

Such, **Sutch**, **Zouch** from Old French, meaning a 'tree-stump'.

Sudbury, **Sudberry** from Old English, meaning a 'southern manor house/fort'.

Sudell from Old English, meaning 'someone who lives in the south dale'.

Suffolk from Old English, meaning 'southern people/the man who comes from the south'.

Sugden from Old English, meaning someone who dwells in a 'swampy valley'.

Summerby, **Somersby** from Old Norse, meaning 'someone who lives on a farm used in the summer'. Similar names include **Summerfield**, **Somerfield** meaning a 'field for use in the summer'; **Summerhill** a 'hill to be used in the summer'; **Summerscale** a 'summer hut', and **Summerton**, **Somerton** meaning a 'farmhouse/homestead that is used in summer'.

Sommers, **Summers** most likely not meaning 'summer' but from Old French, meaning a 'sumpter' – a mule or packhorse – and therefore a name for a muleteer. (*See also* **Sumpter**.)

Sumner from Old French, meaning a 'summoner' (an officer who issues warrants for people to appear in court).

Sumpter, **Sunter** from Old French, meaning a 'driver of a pack-horse'.

Surridge from Old French, meaning a 'southerner/someone from the south'.

Sutcliff, **Sutcliffe** from Old English, meaning 'someone who lives by the south cliff'.

Sutherland from Old Norse, meaning 'south land'.

Sutton from Old English, meaning 'someone who lives on a farm located in the south/south-facing farm'.

Swain, **Swaine** from Old Norse, meaning a 'servant/boy' and used to denote a swineherd.

Swan, **Swann** from Old English, there are two different interpretations of this name. It could mean a 'herdsman/swain', or it could mean a 'swan' as in the bird.

Swanton from Old English, meaning a 'swineherds' place'.

Swart from Old English, meaning 'swarthy'.

Sweatman, **Sweetman** from Old English, meaning a 'sweet man'.

Sweeney, **Swiney** from Irish MacSweeney, meaning 'son of Suibhne' ('pleasant').

Sweet, from Old English, meaning 'sweet' as in 'sweet-natured', a nickname.

Sweeting from Old English, meaning 'sweet/beloved/loved one'.

Swift from Old English, meaning 'swift/fleet of foot'.

Swinburn, **Swinburne** from Old English, meaning a 'pig stream'. Then there is **Swindell** meaning a 'valley with pigs'; **Swinden**, **Swindon** a 'hill with pigs'; **Swinford** a 'pig ford', and **Swinyard** for 'someone who works in the swine yard'.

Swithenbank from Old English, meaning 'a burnt hillside'.

Sword, **Sworder**, **Swords** from Old English, denoting someone who made and/or sold swords.

Sykes, **Sikes** from Old English, meaning a 'stream that flows through marshy ground'.

Taber, **Taberer**, **Tabor** from Old French, meaning a 'drum/ drummer'.

Taberner, **Tabberner** as above – from Old French, meaning a 'drummer'.

Tackley from Old English, meaning a 'pasture for raising young sheep' i.e. tegs.

Taft *see* **Toft**.

Tagge from Old English, meaning a 'young sheep, teg', a nickname.

Tagart, **Taggart** *see* **MacTaggart**.

Tailor *see* **Taylor**.

Tait from Old Norse, meaning 'happy/gay'.

Talbot, **Talbott** most likely from Old French, meaning a 'bandit' or 'robber'.

Talboys, **Tallboy**, **Tallboys** from Old French, meaning 'cut wood' and referring to a woodcutter.

Tancock a diminutive form of 'Andrew' plus 'cock'.

Tancred from Old German, meaning a 'thought counsel'.

Tandy a diminutive form of 'Andrew'.

Tanguy, **Tangye**, **Tinguy** from Breton, meaning a 'fire dog'.

Tanner from Old English, meaning a 'tanner'.

Taper from Old English, meaning a 'taper/wick/candle' and probably referring to a maker of such.

Tapper from Old English, meaning a 'tapper' (of casks) and referring to an inn-keeper.

Tarbuck from Old English, meaning a 'stream/brook in the thorns'.

Tardew from Old French, meaning 'sluggish' and referring to a person of slow nature.

Tarn from Old Norse, meaning a 'pool/small lake'.

Tarrier from Middle English, meaning a 'hunting dog, terrier'.

Tasch from Old English, meaning 'at the ash tree'.

Tasker from Middle English, meaning a 'task-worker'.

Tate, **Tates** from Old English, meaning a 'hilltop'.

Taverner, **Tavernor**, **Tavener**, **Tavenner**, **Tavenor** from Old French, meaning an 'inn-keeper'.

Taylor, **Tayler**, **Tailyour** from Old French, meaning a 'tailor'.

Teal, **Teale** from Middle English, meaning a 'teal' (a water-fowl) and probably first used as a nickname.

Tebb Tebbet, **Tebbett**, **Tebbit** diminutives of 'Theobald'.

Tegg from Old English, meaning a 'young sheep' and referring to someone who herded them. (*See also* **Tagge**.)

Telfer, **Telford** from Old French, meaning 'cut iron' or 'iron-cutter'.

Templar, **Templer** from Old French, a 'member of a military/religious order, consisting of knights whose job it was to protect pilgrims on their way to the Holy Land' hence 'Knight Templar'.

Templeman from Old French, meaning a 'servant of the Templars'.

Tench from Old French, meaning a 'tench', probably a nickname for a fat, sleek person resembling the fish.

Tennant, **Tennent** from Old English, meaning a 'tenant'.

Tennyson, **Tennison** a variant of **Denison** (*see p.41*).

Terrey, **Terry** from Old German meaning 'people rule'.

Tester from Old French, meaning a 'big head'.

Thackeray, **Thackara**, **Thackray** from Old Norse, meaning a 'nook where reeds grow for thatching'.

Thackway from Old Norse, meaning 'someone who lives on land where thatching reeds grow'.

Thatcher from Old English, meaning a 'thatcher of roofs'.

Thelwall, **Thelwell** from Old English, meaning a 'pool by a bridge'.

Theobald, **Theobalds** from Old German, meaning 'people bold'.

Theodore from Greek, meaning 'God's gift'.

Thew, **Thewes** from Old English, meaning a 'servant/slave'.

Thewles, **Thewliss** from Old English, meaning 'rude/ill-mannered'.

Thick from Middle English, meaning 'stout'.

Thin, **Thyne**, **Thynne** from Old English, meaning 'slender/thin'.

Thirsk from Old Norse, meaning a 'lake'.

Thistleton from Old English, meaning a 'place/farm with thistles'.

Thomas an Aramaic name meaning a 'twin'. Before the Conquest this name was confined to priests. Subsequently, however, it became a very popular Christian name, and came to be used as a surname as well, as did diminutives such as **Thom**, **Thoms**, **Tom**, **Tome**, and (double diminutives) **Tomlin**, **Tomlins**, **Tomalin**, **Tomkin**, **Tomkins**; **Tomb**, **Toombes** are also diminutives, but with an intrusive *b*. Then there are all the patronymics: **Thomason**, **Thompson**, **Thomson** and **Tomkinson**. (*See also under* **Mac**.)

Thorburn, **Thurban** from Old Norse, meaning 'Thor-warrior'.

Thorn, **Thorne** from Old English, meaning 'someone who lives near the thornbush/hawthorn'. Thorny surnames include

Thornberry, Thornbery, Thornborough, Thornborrow meaning a 'hill' or 'fort' covered with hawthorn/thornbushes; **Thorn(y)croft** 'someone who lives in the croft among thornbushes'; **Thorndike** 'someone who lives by the ditch where thornbushes grow'; and **Thornton** for a person who dwelt in a 'place with thornbushes'.

Thorogood, Thoroughgood, Thurgood from Old English, meaning 'thorough good', or Old Norse, meaning 'Thor-great'.

Thorp, Thorpe from Old English, meaning a 'dairy farm' and referring to its owner or someone working on it.

Thrale, Thrall from Old Norse, meaning a 'servant'.

Thrasher, Thresher from Old English, meaning 'someone who threshes'.

Threlfall from Old Norse, meaning a 'slave's clearing'.

Thrift from Middle English, meaning 'thrift' – possibly 'virtuous'.

Thrower from Old English, meaning 'to throw' and perhaps referring to a potter or a 'thread-thrower'.

Thrush from Old English, meaning a 'thrush' and perhaps referring to someone with a good/sweet voice.

Thurgar from Old Norse, meaning 'Thor spear'.

Thurkettle from Old Norse, meaning 'Thor's cauldron'.

Thurlow from Old English, meaning a 'burial mound'.

Thurman from Old Norse, meaning 'Thor's wrath'.

Thwaite, Thwaites, Thwaits, Thwaytes, Twaite, Twaites from Old Norse, meaning a 'meadow'.

Tibb a diminutive of 'Theobald'.

Tidey, Tidy from Middle English, meaning 'someone of tidy/good appearance'.

Tiernan from Irish MacTiernan, meaning a 'son of lord'.

Tierney from Irish O'Tierney, meaning a 'descendant of lord'.

Tiffany, **Tiffen**, **Tiffin** from Latin, meaning 'the manifestation of God'.

Tigar from Old German, meaning a 'people spear'.

Tiler, **Tyler**, **Tylor** from Old French, meaning either a 'tile-maker' or 'someone who uses tiles'.

Tiller, **Tilley**, **Tillie**, **Tilly** from Old English, meaning 'someone who tills soil'.

Timberlake from Old English, meaning a 'stream with trees'.

Timmerman from Middle English, meaning 'a man who deals with timber'.

Tindsley, **Tinsley** a toponymic, probably from Tinsley in South Yorkshire

Tinker from Middle English, meaning a 'maker/seller of pots, pans etc'.

Tipson meaning 'son of Tibb/Theobald'.

Tisser from Old French, meaning a 'weaver'.

Titler from Middle English, meaning a 'tell-tale/gossip-monger/tattler'.

Tod, **Todd** from Middle English, meaning a 'fox'. Hence **Todhunter** meaning a 'foxhunter', and **Todman** 'fox man' and probably denoting a foxhunter too.

Toft, **Tofts** from Old Norse, meaning 'someone who lives at the croft'.

Toll, **Tolles** from Old English, meaning a 'small clump of trees'.

Toller, **Tolman** from Old English, meaning a 'tax-gatherer, collector of tolls'.

Tong, **Tonge**, **Tongs**, **Tongue** from Old English, meaning a 'chatterbox', or a 'tongue of land' and referring to someone who lived on one.

Toogood from Old English, meaning 'too good' and probably first used to mock someone.

Took, **Tooke** from the Scandinavian name 'Tóki'.

Tooth from Old English, probably first used as a nickname for someone with prominent teeth.

Toothill, **Tootal**, **Tootle** from Old English, meaning a 'look-out hill' and referring to someone who lived close to one.

Topp from Old Norse, meaning a 'tuft/forelock'.

Topham from Old English, meaning 'someone who lives on a homestead with a look-out post'.

Torr either from Old English, meaning a 'rocky hill-top', or from Old French, meaning a 'bull'.

Toshach, **Toshack**, from Gaelic, meaning 'chief/leader'.

Totman, **Tottman** from Old English, meaning a 'watchman'.

Townend, **Townsend**, **Townshend** from Old English, meaning 'someone who lives at the end of the town/village' etc.

Trafford from Old English, meaning 'someone who lives by a valley ford'.

Trainer, **Treanor**, **Traynor** from Old English, meaning 'a trapper/layer of snares'.

Tranter from Medieval Latin *travetarius* meaning a 'hawker'.

Trapp, **Trappe** from Old English, meaning a 'trap' and denoting a 'trapper' (of animals).

Travers, **Travis**, **Traviss** from Old French, meaning 'crossing a bridge/passing through a gate' and probably referring to a toll-keeper.

Treasure from Old French, meaning 'treasure' and perhaps referring to a treasurer or even a miser.

Tredgett from Middle English, meaning either a 'juggler' or a 'trickster'.

Treddinnick, Tredinnick a Cornish name meaning a 'farm that is fortified'. Treddinick is also a village in Cornwall.

Tree, Treece, Trees from Old English, meaning a 'tree' or 'trees' and probably denoting someone who lived close to a particular tree or group of trees that were for some reason prominent – perhaps because the spot was used as a meeting place.

Trefusis a Cornish name meaning a 'fortified farm'.

Trelawny a Cornish name meaning a 'village with a church'.

Tremain, Tremaine, Tremayne, Truman a Cornish name meaning a 'farm at the stone'.

Trench from Old French, meaning a 'ditch/hollow track'.

Trenchard from Old French, meaning 'to cut' and perhaps referring to a swordsman or a cutter of ditches, etc.

Trenowath a Cornish name meaning a 'new farm'.

Trethowan a Cornish name meaning a 'farm located next to a sandbank'.

Trett from Middle English, meaning 'handsome, graceful'.

Trevelyan a Cornish name meaning a 'mill farm'.

Trew *see* **True**.

Trewin a Cornish name meaning a 'white farm'.

Tricker from Old French, meaning a 'trickster'.

Trickett from Old French, meaning a 'cheat, swindler'.

Trigg, Trigger, Triggs from Old Norse, meaning 'someone who is trustworthy/true'.

Trinder from Old English, meaning 'to twist/turn around' and related to the word for 'spindle', so it was probably applied to someone who turned a wheel or a spinner.

Trippett from Old French, meaning an 'evil trick'.

Trollop, Trollope from Old English, meaning a 'troll-valley' and nothing to do with its modern meaning of 'hussy/harlot'.

Trott, Trotter from Old French, meaning 'to trot' and denoting a runner/messenger.

Trouncer from Old French, meaning a 'maker/seller of cudgels'.

Trowbridge, Troubridge from Old English, meaning 'someone who lives by a wooden bridge'.

True, Trew from Old English, meaning either 'true/faithful', or 'tree'.

Truelove from Old English, meaning 'sweetheart/beloved'.

Trueman, Truman from Old English, meaning a 'true/trusty man'.

Trump, Trumper from Old French, meaning a 'trumpet/trumpeter'.

Truss from Old French, meaning a 'bundle'.

Try, Trye from Middle English, meaning 'excellent/good'.

Tucker, Tuckerman from Old English, meaning a 'fuller' i.e. someone who teased cloth.

Tudor the Welsh form of the name 'Theodore'.

Tulk from Old Norse, meaning a 'man'.

Tumman, Tummon from Old English, meaning a 'villager/town-man'.

Tunnard from Old English, meaning a 'village/town herdsman'.

Tupper from Middle English, meaning either 'someone who worked with rams' or a builder whose work involved 'ramming' or beating a mix of earth, mud and straw with heavy hammers and tools called 'rammers'.

Turnbull from Old English, meaning 'turn bull' and probably originally a nickname for someone of great strength.

Turner, Turnor, Turnour from Old French, meaning 'one who turns and fashions wood/metal', etc.

Turnpenny from Old English, meaning 'someone who turns a penny/a profiteer'.

Turpin from Old Norse, the god 'Thor' plus 'Finn'.

Turpitt from Old English, meaning a 'worker at a turf-pit'.

Turtle from Middle English, meaning a 'turtle dove'.

Tweedale, **Tweddell**, **Tweedle** meaning a 'man from the Tweed valley'.

Twigg, **Twigge** from Old English, meaning a 'slender shoot' and describing a thin man.

Twiner from Middle English, meaning 'someone who twines' (probably thread).

Twitchen, **Twitchin**, **Twitching** from Old English, meaning 'someone who lives at the place where two roads cross/at the crossroads'.

Twyford from Old English, meaning 'someone who lives at the double ford'.

Tye from Old English, meaning an 'enclosed pasture/field, common field'.

Tyson from Old French, meaning a 'firebrand'.

Ubank *see* **Ewbank**.

Ullman, Ullmann, Ulman, Ulmann from Middle English, meaning 'oil' and referring to a maker/seller of oil.

Ullrich, Ulrich *see* **Woolrich**.

Uncle, Uncles from Old Norse, meaning a 'wolf cauldron', but also from Middle English, meaning 'uncle'.

Underdown, Underhill from Old English, meaning someone who lived 'at the bottom of the hill'.

Underwood from Old English, meaning someone who lived 'below a wood'.

Unsworth from Old English, meaning a 'dog enclosure'.

Unthank from Old English, meaning 'without leave' and probably referring to a squatters' settlement.

Unwin from Old English, meaning an 'enemy/foe' (quite literally an 'un-friend').

Upcott from Old English, meaning someone who lived near/in the 'upper cottage'.

Uphill from Old English, meaning someone who lived 'up on a hill'.

Upjohn from Welsh 'ap John', meaning 'son of John'.

Uppington from Old English, meaning 'up in the village'.

Upright from Old English, meaning 'someone with an upright posture/erect/honourable'.

Upton from Old English, meaning 'someone who lives at the upper farm'.

Urban from Latin *urbanus* meaning 'of the city' and therefore denoting a city dweller.

Urquhart meaning 'wood-side'.

Ursell from Latin *ursus* meaning a 'bear'.

Urwin *see* **Erwin**.

Usher from Old French, meaning an 'usher/door-keeper'.

Uttridge *see* **Outridge**.

Vacher from Old French, meaning 'someone who tends to the cows/cowherd'.

Vail *see* **Veil**.

Vaisey, **Vaizey**, **Vasey** from Old French, meaning 'playful'.

Vale, **Vall** from Old French, meaning a 'vale/valley' and denoting someone who lived in one.

Valentin, **Valentine** from Latin meaning 'strong/powerful.'

Valiant, **Vaillant** from Old French, meaning 'courageous'.

Vallet, **Valet** from Old French, meaning a 'valet/manservant'.

Van, **Vann** *see* **Fann**.

Vane *see* **Fane**.

Vanner *see* **Fanner**.

Vantage from Old French, meaning an 'advantage/profit'.

Varder from Old French, meaning a 'verderer' (an official responsible for maintaining law and order in the royal forests).

Varley probably a southern form of **Farley** (*see p.49*).

Vass, **Vasse** from Old French, meaning a 'servant'.

Vassar from Old French, meaning 'vassal'.

Vassall from Middle English, and Old French, meaning a 'servant/dependant'.

Vaughan, **Vaugham** from Old Welsh, meaning 'little/small'.

Vaus, **Vaux** from Old French, meaning a 'valley' and referring to someone who lived in one, or meaning 'false' and referring to a liar.

Veal, **Veale** from Old French, meaning either a 'calf' or 'old'.

Veck from Old French, meaning a 'bishop'.

Veil, **Vail** from Old French, meaning a 'watchman'.

Vender from Old French, meaning 'someone who sells/a tradesman'.

Venn *see* **Fenn**.

Venner either from Old French, meaning a 'huntsman', or from Old English, meaning 'someone who lives on a marsh'.

Venton from Old English, meaning 'someone who lives on a fen farm'.

Verity from Old French, meaning 'truth'.

Verrier from Old French, meaning 'someone who works with glass'.

Verrey, **Verry**, **Verey**, from Old French, meaning 'true'.

Vicar, **Vicker**, **Vickery** from Old French, meaning a 'vicar'.

Vicarage, **Vickerage**, **Vickridge** meaning a 'servant of the vicary/vicar'.

Vicars, **Vickars**, **Vickers** meaning either 'the vicar's servant' or 'the vicar's son'.

Vidler *see* **Fidler**.

Villar, **Villars**, **Villiers** from Old French, meaning a 'part of a village/farm'.

Vincent, **Vincett**, **Vincen**, **Vinson** from Latin meaning 'conquering'; **Vince** is a diminutive form of this name.

Vine, **Vines** from Old French, meaning a 'vine/vineyard' and denoting someone who either lived or worked on/near one.

Vinter, **Vintor** from Old French, meaning a 'vintner/wine merchant'.

Virgin from Latin meaning a 'virgin' and denoting a man who played the Blessed Virgin in a mystery play.

Vise, **Vize** from Old French, meaning 'someone who lived close to a boundary'.

Vivian, **Vivians** most likely from Latin *vivianus* meaning 'living'.

Vizard *see* **Wishart**.

Voller, **Vollers** *see* **Fuller**.

Voyle from Old Welsh, meaning 'bald-headed' and given as a nickname.

Waddell of uncertain origin but probably derived from places with a similar name – Wadden Hall in Waltham (which could perhaps come from Old English, meaning 'wood enclosure', or Middle English, meaning 'wooden hall'), or from Wedale in Midlothian.

Wade from Old English, meaning 'to go', or meaning someone who dwelt by a 'ford'. 'Wade' was also the name of a sea giant.

Wadsworth, **Wordsworth** from Old English, meaning a 'farm/homestead of Wade'.

Waghorn, **Waghorne** from Old English, meaning 'to wield a horn' and perhaps applied to a trumpeter.

Wagstaff, **Wagstaffe** from Old English, probably applied to a beadle/officer of the law.

Waight *see* **Wait**.

Wain, **Waine**, **Wayne** from Old English, meaning a 'cart/wain' and denoting either a maker or a seller of these vehicles.

Wainer from Old English, meaning a 'wagon driver'.

Wainewright, **Wainright**, **Wainwright** from Old English, meaning 'someone who makes wagons'.

Waistell *see* **Wastell**.

Wait, **Waight**, **Waite**, **Waites** from Old French, meaning a 'watchman', probably of a fortified town (an occupation that was combined with that of musician).

Wake from Old Norse, meaning someone who was 'alert'.

Wakeham from Old English, meaning either 'someone who roused people from their sleep' or, less likely, a 'meadow belonging to Wake'.

Wakeman from Middle English, meaning a 'watchman/someone who would keep vigil'.

Walbank, **Wallbank** from Old English, meaning 'someone who lives by the bank of the stream'.

Walbrook, **Wallbrook** from Old English, meaning 'someone who lives by the stream'.

Walby, **Walbey** from Old English, meaning a 'farm/village built on/next to the Roman wall'.

Wald, **Walde**, **Weld**, **Wold** from Old English, meaning someone who lived 'in woods or a forest'.

Waldman from Old English, meaning 'someone who lives in a forest'.

Wale from Middle English, meaning 'excellent', or from Old English, meaning 'someone who lives by the ridge'.

Walford from Old English, meaning a 'ford with a stream' and probably denoting someone who lived close by.

Walker from Old English, meaning a 'fuller' (i.e. someone who treads on cloth in the process of fulling).

Walkman this is a variation of the name **Wakeman**, i.e. a watchman.

Wall from Old English, meaning 'someone who lived near to a wall' and probably referring to a seawall or the wall surrounding a city or town.

Wallace a Scots form of **Wallis** (*see below*), usually referring to a Briton of Strathclyde.

Waller there are several possible meanings to this name. It can come from Old English, meaning 'someone who lives by a wall', or it may mean 'someone who lives by the stream'. Alternatively, from

Middle English, it could mean 'someone who builds walls/a bricklayer' or a 'salt-weller'.

Wallis from Anglo-French, meaning a 'Welshman/Celt/foreigner'.

Walmesley, **Walmsley** from Old English, meaning a 'lake in a wood'.

Walpole from Old English, meaning 'someone who lives by a pool by a wall'.

Walsh, **Walshe** from Old English, meaning 'Welsh' or 'foreigner'.

Walter from Old German, meaning 'mighty army'. It has spawned several other surnames: **Walters** and **Waterson** meaning 'son of Walter'. **Watkin**, **Watkins Watt**, **Watts** as diminutives, and their patronymics, **Watkinson** and **Watson**.

Walwin, **Walwyn** from Old English, meaning a 'power-friend'.

Wanless, **Wanliss**, **Wandloss** from Middle English, meaning 'luckless'.

Wann from Middle English, meaning 'pale/wan'.

Want, **Whant** from Middle English, meaning a 'mole' and denoting a mole-catcher, or meaning someone who lived by the 'crossroads'.

Waple from Old English, meaning 'wield pole/wag staff'.

Warboy, **Warboys** from Old French, meaning 'guard woods' possibly referring to a forester.

Ward, **Warde** from Old English, meaning a 'watchman/guard', or possibly from Middle English, meaning 'someone who lived or worked in marshland'.

Wardel *see* **Wardle**.

Warden from Old French, meaning a 'guardian/warden'.

Wardle, **Wardel** from Old English, meaning a 'look-out hill/watch-hill'.

Wardman from Middle English, meaning a 'marshman' and denoting someone who worked in a marsh, or the name could also mean a 'watchman'.

Ware from Old English, meaning 'cautious/wary', or meaning a 'weir' and referring to someone who worked or lived on a weir.

Wareham from Old English, denoting someone who lived on a 'homestead near a weir'.

Waring, **Wearing** from the popular Norman name 'Warin' (found in French in the form 'Guérin').

Warlock, **Worlock** from Old English, meaning a 'traitor/enemy/devil'.

Warman from Old English, either meaning a 'merchant', or a 'faith-protector'.

Warme from Old English, meaning 'warm' but probably referring to someone with religious fervour/a zealot.

Warner from the Norman name 'Warin', meaning 'Warin army', or from Old French, meaning 'warrener/gamekeeper'.

Warr from Old French, meaning 'war' and probably referring to a soldier.

Warrener, **Warrender**, **Warriner** from Old French, meaning a 'keeper of game'.

Warrington from Old English, meaning 'someone who lives at a farm by the weir'.

Warton from Old English, meaning a 'look-out post'.

Warwick the most likely source of this name is Old English, for a 'dairy farm located by or near a weir'.

Washer from Old English, and probably denoting a washer of clothes.

Washington from Old English, meaning a 'family farm/homestead'.

Wasp, **Waspe** from Old English, meaning a 'wasp' and perhaps first used as a nickname.

Wastell, **Waistell** from Old French, meaning a 'cake/bread made from finest flour' and probably referring to a maker/seller of these.

Watchman from Old English, meaning just what it says.

Water, Waters this name derives from the medieval way of pronouncing 'Walter' but can also derive from Old English for 'water', referring to someone who lived close to a source of water.

Waterer from Old English, meaning either a 'water-seller' or someone who 'irrigates' land, or waters farm animals.

Waterhouse from Old English, meaning 'someone who lives in the house by the water'.

Waterman from Old English, meaning a 'carrier of water or someone who sells water'. On occasion it might also refer to a 'boatman'.

Watman *see* **Whatman**.

Watmough, Whatmaugh, Whatmore probably from Middle English, meaning 'Wat's brother/son/brother in law' (or possibly some other male relative of Wat, or Walter).

Waugh from Old English, meaning 'foreigner'.

Waxman from Old English, meaning a 'maker/seller of wax'.

Way, Waye, Wey from Old English, meaning a 'road/pathway'.

Waycott from Old English, meaning 'someone who lives in the cottage by the roadside'.

Waylatt from Old English, meaning 'someone who lives at the crossroads'.

Wayre from Old English, meaning 'someone who lives by the stream/bathing pool'.

Wear, Weare, Weir from Old English, meaning a 'weir/dam' and denoting someone who lived near such a place.

Weather, Weathers from Old English, meaning a 'wether' i.e. a neutered sheep, and probably referring to the person who looked after them.

Weatherby *see* **Wetherby**.

Weaver, Weavers from Old English, meaning a 'weaver'.

Webb, Webbe, Webber from Old English, meaning a 'weaver'.

Webster from Old English, meaning a 'female weaver' although in Middle English this name was used more often for men.

Wedlake, Widlake from Old English, meaning a 'wide stream/wide stretch of water'.

Wedmore from Old English, meaning a 'moor/hunting ground'.

Weech, Week, Weekes *see* **Wich**.

Weinberg from Old German, meaning a 'vineyard' and denoting someone who lived or worked on one.

Weir *see* **Wear**.

Welbourn, Welbon, Welburn from Old English, meaning a 'stream issuing from a spring'.

Welch *see* **Welsh**.

Welcome, Wellcome, Willicombe from Old English, meaning 'welcome' or on occasion 'well-kept'. It could also refer to someone who dwelt in a 'valley with a spring'.

Weldon from Old English, meaning 'someone who lives near a hill with a stream'.

Welfare, Wellfare from Old English, meaning a 'well-faring' person i.e. a prosperous man.

Welland from Old Welsh and Old English, meaning someone who lived 'on land next to the river/stream'.

Wellbeloved from Old English, a nickname for a very well-liked person.

Weller from Old English, meaning either 'someone who lives by the stream/spring', or 'someone who works with salt/a salt-boiler'.

Wellman from Old English, meaning 'someone who lives by the spring or the stream'.

Wells, Welles from Old English, meaning 'one who dwells by a spring or springs' (*see also* **Attwell**, *under* **Attenborough**).

Wellstead from Old English, meaning 'someone who lives by a spring or the head of a stream'.

Welsh, **Welch**, **Wellish** from Old English, meaning 'Welsh/Celtic/foreign'.

Wemyss, **Weems** from Scots Gaelic, for 'caves', probably a name given to a man from Wemyss in Fife.

Wenn from Old English, meaning a 'wart' and often used to denote a hillock or mound of earth – so a name given to someone who dwelt on or by such a landmark.

Wensley from Old English, meaning 'Woden's wood'.

Went, **Whent** from Middle English, meaning a 'crossroad/path'.

Wentworth most likely from Old English, meaning either a 'worth' ('homestead/ enclosure') that can be occupied during winter, or a 'worth that is owned by Winter'.

Wesker from Middle English, meaning someone living near the 'west fenland'.

West from Old English, meaning 'someone who lives to the west of a certain place' or 'man from the west'. Other westerly names include **Westbrook** meaning someone from 'west of the brook' or 'who lived close to the western brook'; **Westbroom** meaning 'someone who lived/came from west of the gorse/broom'; **Westbury** someone from 'the western fort/house' or 'to the west of the fort/house'; **Westcott**, **Westacott** someone who lives in the 'west cottage'; **Western** meaning 'someone from the west'; **Westfield** 'someone from the west field/who lives close to the west field'; **Westgate** 'someone who lives by the west gate'; **Westhall** 'someone who lives in/by the west enclosure'; **Westlake** 'someone who lives by the west lake/stream'; **Westman** 'man from the west'; **Weston** someone from 'the west farm/the west-facing farm' or 'to the west of the farm'; **Westover** from the 'western slope'; **Westward** meaning 'someone who lives to the west', and **Westwood** 'someone who lives in the west wood/the west-facing wood'.

Wetherall, Wetherhill, Weatherill from Old English, meaning a 'sheep enclosure', and denoting someone who lived near one or who tended the wethers, or someone who came from a place of that name.

Wetherbee, Wetherby, Weatherby from Old Norse, meaning 'someone who lives on/by a farm with wethers' (neutered sheep).

Wetherhead from Old English, meaning a 'shepherd' i.e. a herder of wethers (neutered sheep).

Wetter from Old English, meaning 'someone who lives by water'.

Wetton from Old English, meaning a 'wet hill'

Weyman, Wyman, Wymann, Wymans from Old English, meaning 'war/battle protection'.

Whakum see Wakeham.

Whale, Whales from Old English, and Middle English, meaning a 'whale' and denoting someone who was very large!

Wharf, Wharfe from Old English, meaning a 'wharf' and probably denoting someone who worked on one.

Whateley, Whately, Whatley, Wheatley meaning 'wheatfield'.

Whatman, Watman from Old English, meaning a 'brave man'.

Whatmoor from Old English, meaning a 'damp/clammy moor'.

Wheadon from Old English, meaning 'someone who dwells near a wheat hill/wheat valley'.

Wheat, Wheate from Old English, meaning someone 'brave/bold'.

Wheatcroft from Old English, meaning someone dwelling in or by a 'croft where wheat grows'. Similarly, **Wheatfill** means 'someone who lives by a wheatfield', and **Wheatland** 'someone who lives close to wheat land'.

Wheel, Wheele from Old English, meaning a 'wheel' and denoting someone who lived by a 'waterwheel' or who was in charge of the waterwheel.

Wheeler, Wheelwright from Old English, meaning a 'maker of wheels'.

Whinney from Old English, meaning 'someone who lives on/near a whin-covered hill' (i.e. covered in furze or gorse).

Whistler from Old English, meaning a 'piper'.

Whitaker, Whittaker from Old English, meaning 'someone who lives by the white field/wheat field'.

Whitbourn, Whitbourne from Old English, meaning either 'someone who lives by the white stream' or a 'fair-haired child'.

Whitbread from Old English, meaning 'white bread' or 'wheat bread' and denoting a maker/seller of it.

Whitburn from Old English, meaning 'someone who lives by the white stream'.

Whitby from Old Norse, meaning a 'white town'.

Whitcher, Whicher from Old English, meaning 'someone who makes chests' although it can also derive from another Old English word and refer to a 'dairy farmer'.

Whitcomb, Whitcombe from Old English, meaning 'someone who lives in a wide valley'.

White, Whitt, Whyte Witt most often from Old English, for 'white' or 'fair' but sometimes it refers to 'someone who lives by a bend or curve in a road'.

Whitefield, Whitfield from Old English, meaning someone who lives by a 'white field' and probably referring to chalky or limed soil although some researchers have suggested it could also mean 'open pastureland'.

Whitehead from Old English, meaning 'someone with white or fair hair'.

Whitehill from Old English, meaning either 'someone who lived close to a white hill' or to a 'hollow in a hillside'.

Whitehorn, **Whithorn** from Old English, meaning someone who owned a 'bright trumpet or splendid drinking horn'.

Whitehouse, **Whithouse** from Old English, meaning 'someone who lived at the white house'.

Whitelaw from Old English, meaning 'someone who lives on a white hill'. Whitelaw is also the name of places near both Kelso and Melrose in the Borders of Scotland.

Whiteley, **Whitely** from Old English, meaning a 'white clearing'.

Whiteman, **Whitman** from Old English, meaning a 'white/fair-headed man'.

Whitesmith from Old English, meaning a 'whitesmith/tinsmith'.

Whiteway from Old English, meaning 'someone who lives next to a white road'.

Whiting meaning a 'son of White'.

Whitmarsh from Old English, meaning 'someone who lives by the white marsh' (i.e. the chalky marsh).

Whitney from Old English, meaning a 'white island' and denoting someone who lived on one.

Whittier from Old English, meaning 'someone who dresses skins to make white leather'.

Whittington from Old English, meaning 'someone who lives at the white farm/white homestead'.

Whittle from Old English, meaning a 'white hill' and denoting someone who lived on/by one.

Whitworth from Old English, meaning 'White's Worth' or from places named Whitworth in Durham and Lancashire.

Wich, **Wick**, **Wicke**, **Wickes**, **Wicks**, **Wych**, **Wyche**, **Weech**, **Week**, **Weekes** from Old English, meaning a 'dwelling place/home' or a 'village', but was later used to meaning a 'dairy-farm' (as in Butterwick, Chiswick). **Wich/Wych** may also mean someone who lived 'by a wych elm'.

Wicken, **Wickens**, **Wicker**, **Wickers** from Old English, meaning 'someone who lived/worked on a dairy farm'.

Wickham, **Wykeham** from Old English, meaning either a 'homestead with a dairy farm' or a 'homestead by a meadow'.

Widdecombe, **Widdicombe** from Old English, meaning someone who lived in a 'withy (willow) valley'.

Widdowes, **Widdows**, **Widders** from Old English, meaning a 'widow', and extended to mean 'widower'. Hence **Widdowson**, **Widderson** meaning 'the widow's son'.

Widger from Old English, meaning 'elf spear'.

Widmer from Old English, meaning 'dweller by a pool in the willow trees'.

Wigg from Old English, meaning a 'beetle' and probably first used as a nickname.

Wight either from Middle English, meaning 'someone strong/able' or referring to someone from the Isle of Wight.

Wightman from Old English, meaning 'elf man', or Middle English, meaning 'strong man'.

Wilber from Old English, meaning 'wild boar'.

Wilberforce probably from Wilberfoss ('wild-boar ditch'?) in Yorkshire, denoting someone who came from there.

Wilby from Old English and Old Norse, meaning 'dweller/worker on a willow farm'.

Wild, **Wilde** from Old English, meaning 'wild/violent' or sometimes referring to 'uncultivated land/wild land'.

Wildblood from Old English, meaning 'wild blood' and no doubt referring to someone with a wild nature.

Wilder from Old English, meaning a 'wild animal.'

Wilding from Old English, meaning 'wild one'.

Wildman from Old English, meaning a 'wild man'.

Wiles from Old English, meaning a 'fish-trap' and denoting trickery.

Wiley, Wylie from either Old English, meaning a 'clearing' or from Middle English, meaning someone 'wily'.

Wilfred from Old English, meaning 'will-peace'.

Willer from Old English, meaning a 'basket' and referring to someone who made/sold them.

Willgrass from Old Norse, meaning a 'wild pig' and no doubt first used as a nickname.

Williams from Old German, the name 'William', meaning 'will helmet', was extremely popular after the Conquest, and came to be used, in various forms, as a surname. **Williamson** is obviously 'son of William'; then there are pet names and diminutives and double diminutives: **Wilcock, Wilcox, Wilk, Wilke, Wilkes, Wilkie Will, Willis** and **Wilkin, Willat, Willats, Willet, Willetts,** and their 'sons': **Wilkinson** and **Wilkerson,** and **Wilson** (one of the commonest surnames in the British Isles).

Willock, Willocks, Willox from Old English, meaning a 'battle creature'.

Willoughby from Old English and Old Norse, meaning 'someone who dwells in a farm by the willows'.

Willows from Old English, meaning 'willows' and referring to someone who lived close to these trees.

Wimple from Old English, meaning a 'maker/seller of wimples'.

Wimbolt, Winbolt from Old English, meaning 'friend-bold'.

Winch, Wynch, Winks from Old English, meaning a 'pulley/winch' and no doubt referring to someone who operated one. 'Winch' can also mean a 'sharp bend in a river or a valley'.

Wind, Wynde from Old English, probably a nickname for someone who was as fast as the wind, or it could mean one who dwelt near or along a 'winding path'.

Windebank from Old English, meaning one who lived on a 'windy hill'.

Winder from Old English, meaning a 'winder' (probably of wool yarn).

Window, **Windows**, **Windus** from Old English, meaning 'someone who worked in a winding house, a winder of yarn'.

Windsor from Old English, meaning a 'riverbank with a winch' (possibly for drawing up boats). Windsor has been the surname of the British Royal family since 1917.

Windus *see* **Windows**.

Wine, **Wyne** from Old English, meaning a 'friend'.

Wingar, **Winger** from Old English, meaning a 'friend spear'.

Wingate from Old English, meaning 'someone who lives in a windy thoroughfare/pass'.

Wingfield from Old English, meaning a 'pastureland'.

Winn from Old English, meaning a 'friend'.

Winston, **Winstone** from Old English, meaning a 'joy stone' or a 'friend's farm'.

Winter, **Winters**, **Wintour**, **Wynter**, **Wynters** from Old English, meaning 'winter' and denoting someone who was born during this season or someone with white hair.

Winterbotham, **Winterbottom** from Old English, meaning 'someone who lives in a cold dell'.

Winterton from Old English, meaning a 'farm in winter'.

Winyard, **Wynyard** from Old English, meaning 'someone who worked in the vineyard'.

Wiseman from Old English, meaning a 'wise man' but the name might also apply to a 'juggler' or have been applied in jest to a fool.

Wish from Old English, meaning 'someone who lives in a marshy/damp field/meadow'.

Wishart, **Vizard** from Old Norse, meaning 'wise'.

Wither, **Withers** from Old English, meaning 'someone who lives by the willows'. Similarly, **Witheridge** means 'someone who lives by a ridge of willows', and **Withey**, **Withy** 'someone who lives by the willow(s)'.

Witty, **Wittey** from Old English, meaning 'witty/wise'.

Wogan from Welsh, meaning a 'scowl or frown'. A name found in Ireland since the thirteenth century.

Wold *see* **Wald**.

Wolf, **Wolfe**, **Woolf**, **Woolfe** from Old English, meaning a 'wolf'.

Wolfenden most likely from Old English, meaning 'an enclosure for keeping out wolves'.

Wolsey, **Woolsey** from Old English, meaning 'wolf victory'.

Wood, **Woods**, **Wode** from Old English, meaning a 'wood', but occasionally from another Old English word meaning 'frenzied'.

Woodbridge from Old English, meaning 'someone who lived by the wooden bridge'. Also refers to towns in the counties of Dorset and Suffolk.

Woodchurch from Old English, meaning 'dweller by the wooden church'.

Woodcock from Old English, meaning a 'woodcock' and probably first used as a nickname. The woodcock is a bird known for its stupidity.

Woodcraft, **Woodcroft** from Old English, meaning 'someone who lives at the croft near the wood'.

Woodend from Old English, meaning 'dweller at the end of the wood'.

Woodey from Old English, meaning 'someone who lives in an enclosure in the wood'.

Woodfall from Old English, meaning 'someone who lives near a fold (perhaps of sheep?) in the wood.

Woodford, **Woodforde** from Old English, meaning 'someone who lives by the ford in the wood'.

Woodgate from Old English, meaning 'someone who lives by the gate to the wood'.

Woodhall, **Woodall** from Old English, meaning 'someone who lives in a hall in the wood'.

Woodham from Old English, meaning 'someone who lives in a village/homestead/enclosure in the wood'.

Woodhead from Old English, meaning 'someone who lives at the top of the wood.'

Woodhouse, **Wodehouse** from Old English, meaning 'someone who lives in the house in the wood'.

Woodier, **Woodyer**, **Woodger** from Old English, meaning 'someone who works/cuts wood' i.e. a woodcutter.

Woodland from Old English, meaning 'someone who lives in the woodland'.

Woodley from Old English, meaning 'someone who lives in a clearing/glade in the wood'.

Woodman from Old English, meaning a 'woodman'.

Woodrow from Old English, meaning 'someone who lives in a row of cottages/huts in a wood'.

Woodside from Old English, meaning 'someone who lives by the woodside'.

Woodstock from Old English, meaning 'someone who lives in a place in the wood'.

Woodward from Old English, meaning a 'keeper of the wood/forester'.

Wooley *see* **Woolley**.

Woolgar, **Woolger** from Old English, meaning a 'wolf spear'.

Woolhouse from Old English, meaning 'someone who works at a house that stores wool'.

Wooll, **Woolls** from Old English, meaning a 'pool/well' and denoting someone who lived by one.

Woolland, **Woollan**, **Woollon** there are two different meanings to this name from Old English, 'someone who lives on/near pastureland', or 'someone who lives near curved land'.

Woollard from Old English, meaning a 'wolf ward/guardian'.

Wooler from Old English, meaning 'someone who buys/sells or works with wool'.

Woolley, **Wooley** from Old English, meaning 'wolves' wood/dwelling' although sometimes it also means a 'wolf hill' or a 'clearing by a stream/rivulet'.

Woolman from Old English, meaning a 'wool-man/merchant of wool'.

Woolmer from Old English, meaning 'wolf famous' or referring to a 'pool round which wolves drink' or a 'moor upon which wolves live'.

Woolner, **Woolnoth** from Old English, meaning 'wolf bold'.

Woolrich, **Woolridge**, **Ullrich**, **Ulrich** from Old English, meaning 'wolf powerful'.

Woolston, **Woolstone**, **Wolstone** from Old English, meaning 'wolf stone'.

Woolton from Old English, meaning 'Wolf's farm'.

Woolven from Old English, meaning 'wolf friend'.

Woolverton, **Wolverton** from Old English, meaning 'Wolf's settlement'.

Wooton, **Wootton** from Old English, meaning a 'someone who lives/works in a farm by a wood'.

Wordsworth *see* **Wadsworth**.

Work, **Worke** from Old English, meaning 'work' or 'fortification'.

Worker Workman from Old English, meaning 'to work' and denoting a worker of any type.

Worlock *see* **Warlock**.

Worm, Worms from Old English, meaning a 'snake/reptile/dragon'.

Wormley from Old English, meaning 'someone who lives in a clearing with snakes, reptiles etc'.

Woral, Worrall, Worrell meaning 'someone who lives near a place with bog-myrtle'.

Worth from Old English, meaning an 'enclosure/homestead'.

Worthing from Old English, meaning 'someone worthy'.

Worthington from Old English, meaning a 'farm belonging to the family' and therefore denoting someone who lived on it or close by.

Worthy from Old English, meaning either 'an enclosure' or 'worthy' (though less likely to be the latter).

Wray *see* **Wroe**.

Wren, Wrenn from Old English, meaning a 'wren' and either denoting someone who was very small or someone with a beautiful voice.

Wright, Wrighte from Old English, meaning a 'craftsman/carpenter' i.e. anyone who 'wrought/made' things.

Wroe, Wray from Old English, meaning 'someone who lived in a nook/isolated locality'.

Wroth from Old English, meaning 'fierce/angry'.

Wyatt, Guyat a diminutive of 'Guy', though it can also occasionally be a diminutive of 'William'. **Wyatt** may alternatively come from an older name 'Wyartt, Wyard', which comes from Old English, and means 'war-brave'.

Wyber, Wyberg, Wybrow, Whybrow from Old English, meaning a 'war fortress'.

Yale from Old Welsh, meaning a dweller in 'cultivated upland'.

Yalland, Yellond, Yolland from Old English, meaning one who lived in 'ancient/old/cultivated land'.

Yapp from Old English, meaning either 'crooked' or 'shrewd/clever'.

Yard, Yarde from Old English, meaning 'thirty acres/virgate', meaning one who held that much land.

Yardley, Yeardley from Old English, meaning a 'clearing in a wood'. **Yarwood** probably has the same meaning.

Yate, Yates, Yeate, Yeats from Old English, meaning a 'gate' and referring to someone who lived close to a gate or to a gate-keeper.

Yeo, Yea from Old English, meaning a 'river or stream' and referring to some who resided next to one.

Yeoman from Middle English, meaning a 'yeoman' or a 'servant to a nobleman'.

Yong, Yonge, Young, Younge from Old English, meaning 'young', probably a nickname to distinguish between two people of the same name.

Yonwin from Old English, meaning a 'young friend/companion'.

Youle, Yule from Old English, meaning 'someone born/christened at yuletide'.

Younger from Old English, meaning 'junior'.

Younghusband from Old English, meaning a 'young farmer'.

Youngman from Old English, meaning a 'young man/servant'.

Youngmay from Old English, meaning a 'young lad/young servant'.

Zebedee from Hebrew meaning 'my gift'.

Zeller *see* **Sellar.**

Zimmerman from Old German, meaning a 'carpenter'.

Zouch *see* **Such.**

Select Bibliography

G. F. Black, *The Surnames of Scotland* (New York, New York Public Library, 1946; reprinted 1963; new edition, Canongate, 1999)

Basil Cottle, *The Penguin Dictionary of Surnames* (London, Penguin Books, 1978)

R. A. McKinley, *A History of British Surnames* (London, Longman Group Ltd, 1990)

MacLysaght, Edward, *The Surnames of Ireland* (Irish Academic Press, sixth edition, 1985)

James Pennethorne Hughes, *How You Got Your Name* (London, J. M. Dent & Sons, 1963)

P. H. Reaney, *A Dictionary of British Surnames*, with corrections and additions by R. M. Wilson (London, Routledge & Kegan Paul, 1976; third edition, Oxford University Press, 1997)

Ernest Weekly, *The Romance of Names* (London, 1922)